Praise for

Rituals, Poem:

"Have you ever felt the whisper of a

us to uncover that inner knowing, c

nature. This bilingual gem is a heartfelt invitation to discover how everyday acts—from cooking to crystal work—can awaken our innate gifts in a journey back to our *corazón*."

— Ana Flores, Founder of We All Grow Latina

"With *My Little Spiritual Book,* poet and wise woman Annie Vazquez has once again gifted us an exquisite collection filled with the words our hearts most long to hear. Whether you come to these lyrical pages yearning for healing, comfort or joyful inspiration, Annie's soulful words and wisdom are here to help guide your journey. Grab a copy for yourself, your *amigas* and all the loving soul sisters in your life. "

— Alejandra Ramos, TODAY Show Contributor and Host of The Great American Recipe on PBS

"A comprehensive and varied collection of teachings from one of the most humble and talented people I know. Whether you cherry-pick what works for you or immerse yourself in Annie's guides to life, this book will serve you well. Eye-opening and essential."

— Alex Segura, Bestselling and Acclaimed Author of *Secret Identity* and *Alter Ego*

"Annie Vazquez once again proves her vast knowledge when it comes to her craft. The book focuses expertly on the art of self-care for women who, at times, might find themselves busy and putting themselves second, especially when it comes to taking care of their emotional and spiritual well-being. With easy-to-follow content, years of Annie's teachings as well as new lessons come to life in a perfectly packaged tome, with new additions such as self-love exercises, a look at the best plants to lift the energy in one's space, and even cooking tips to keep the home and the heart protected and at peace. A book meant to help readers attract beauty and keep positivity in their lives, this is one meant for the curious and the hopeful."

— Aurora Dominguez, Journalist and Educator

"This book touches on so many layers of the woman's healing journey from the inside out, and every piece of advice and story within it connects and resonates, especially for those people who come from a home where Spanish is the dominant language. More mindfulness and healing are needed in our communities, and the teachings in every chapter provide exactly that."

— Cata Balzano, Multi-Media Journalist

"*My Little Spiritual Book* is a perfect blend of simplicity and depth, making it accessible to spiritual beginners while also providing rich insights for seasoned practitioners. Its easy-to-read format invites you to explore your spiritual journey with grace and intention, making it an essential companion for anyone seeking to deepen their connection with the divine."

— Jo' Martinez, Creatrix of Despojitos MIAMI

"Living with Endometriosis, I often forget to breathe during moments of intense pain and discomfort. In *My Little Spiritual Book*, Annie Vazquez, known as "Miami's Jedi," reminds me to pause and pray for healing, or simply to acknowledge that my body deserves rest. She emphasizes the importance of normalizing prayer for menstrual pain, offering a powerful reminder of the care we should give ourselves in those moments."

— Lucy Lopez, Host of The Mamacita Rica Podcast

"This book is a beautiful compilation of everything you need to know to begin your spiritual journey or deepen it. It encompasses a collection of practices to use in various rituals and guidance for any inner journey you are currently working through or may face in the future. My favorite part of the book is the balance section, where you really get to learn about yin and yang energy."

— Rebecca Arroyo, Mental Health Therapist

"'Stay inspired and full of faith.' These are the words of the iconic writer, entrepreneur and edu-influencer, Annie Vazquez, that perfectly capture the spirit and service of her new book, *My Little Spiritual Book: Rituals, Poems & Practices for Enlightenment*. From helping readers to think about their goals in new ways—"as blooming flowers"—to using everyday symbols, such as the broom and scissors to literally sweep one's room and reshape one's life, Annie has assembled a robust and comprehensive blueprint for love and self-care for daily use, ever reminding us that that magic of our lives is in the everyday commitment to self."

— Shirley Velasquez, Wellness Writer and Former Oprah Daily Editor

"As I read the first page, I was captivated. I couldn't put this magical book down. I felt like this was written just for me. The entire book is filled with so much insight. If you're looking for a book that speaks to your soul, is filled with divine wisdom and true spiritual alchemy, this is it—an absolute must-read."

— Tiffany Arocha, Owner and Spiritual Consultant at Soul II Soul Spiritual Boutique in Miami.

"In my therapy practice, I focus a lot on helping women become empowered, overcome the chains that are keeping them down, and to roar with their voice. *My Little Spiritual Book* is a wonderful tool I can recommend to all my clients so that they can integrate what they have learned in our sessions with the empowerment that this book will give them."

— Taimara Dietsch, MS, LMHC

"From her poems to her gentle ways of sharing lessons about magic, I was hooked from the first word. Annie's words flowed through me like sipping a warm cup of tea on a cold winter day. I felt validated and seen in the parts where she shared her deepest traumas like 'Why I Never Married.' It made me take deep sighs and praise out loud. This book is pure magic. Annie pours herself into this book so readers can pour into themselves and heal."

— Zayda Rivera, Journalist and Spiritual Teacher

MY LITTLE SPIRITUAL BOOK

RITUALS, POEMS & PRACTICES FOR ENLIGHTENMENT

ANNIE VAZQUEZ

Edited by Flor Ana Mireles

1st Edition | 01
Hardcover ISBN: 979-8-9912164-2-5

First Published November 2024

Also available in:
Paperback: 979-8-9912164-5-6

For inquiries and bulk orders, please email:
indieearthpublishinghouse@gmail.com

Printed in the United States of America 1 2 3 4 5 6 7 8 9

Indie Earth Publishing Inc.
| Miami, FL |

www.indieearthbooks.com

INDIE EARTH
PUBLISHING

My Little Spiritual Book

Rituals, Poems & Practices
for Enlightenment

Written by Annie Vazquez

Illustrated by Sol Cotti

To all the wise women who have shown us that
the only way "out" is "in," and that through grace and faith
we can overcome anything as long as we follow our true compass:
our **heart**—our ***corazón***.

A todas las mujeres sabias que nos han demostrado que
la única "salida" es "adentro" y que a través de la gracia y la fe
podemos superar cualquier cosa siempre que sigamos
nuestra verdadera brújula:
nuestro ***corazón***—nuestro **heart**.

Table of Contents

My Little Spiritual Book

The Purpose Of This Book

We are all wise women. Sometimes we just need to connect with our soul a little more to unlock our wisdom within. This interactive book combines the language of my ancestors and the one I learned to first speak: Spanish. Within the contents of this book are a collection of rituals, practices and enlightenment exercises I have shared over the last 7 years on social media and through in-person workshops. Plus, there are lots of first-ever shared materials, including poems, quotes and anecdotes.

The book is divided into 3 chapters each representing the stages we women grow through. It is my ancestors' interpretation of the triple goddesses. **Sage** is the chapter when we learn the art of letting go like a **Full Moon**.

Lavender Oil is the chapter where we have graduated and become master manifestors by using tools like lavender oil, totems and inner child work. We are also more trusting and open to the magic of new beginnings like a **New Moon**.

The last chapter is called **Wise Women** because this is our last stage as women when we have become the most potent in our power. Life has taught us so much and we share these lessons with our loved ones. Sometimes by becoming medicine women. We are highly psychic and able to truly savor the moments. The past, present and future are happening simultaneously which also means you may experience parts of these 3 stages at once.

I hope this book inspires you to connect to your roots, too.

-Annie

3 Ways To Use This Book

1. Use this book in your **morning ritual** before starting your day.
Read a page a day for **inspiration.**
Pencil in your thoughts and fill this book with your **wisdom.**

2. Use this book in your **evening ritual** before going to bed.
This will allow you to **relax** and **rest** well.
Read a page a day.
Write in your thoughts and finish the day with some **enlightenment.**

3. Lastly, simply pick up this book at **any time** to find
a passage or ritual that you need for the **present moment.**

This chapter is all about releasing what no longer serves us just like **sage**, or ***salvia***, which is used in a Full Moon ritual to transmute energy. We begin here because it is the first stage of the triple goddesses when she must learn that life is temporary and we can only hold moments in our hearts not in our hands forever. In this chapter, we explore the art of letting go and how when we close one door, 10 more can fling open with the abundance we truly desire. We connect with the Full Moon in this section.

"She smells like **sage and lavender oil.**
She is a **wise woman.**"

"Huele a **salvia y a aceite de lavanda.**
Es una **mujer sabia.**"

She Is Me And She Is You

She smells like **sage** and **lavender oil.**
Her **crystals** are always **close** by wherever she goes.
In her **pockets**, in her **purse**, in her **pillowcases.**
She talks to her **plants** and **prays** when nobody is watching.
Sometimes, it's a **plea.** Sometimes, it's **gratitude**, and sometimes, it's for **you.**
She practices **meditation**, and on other nights, lights **candles**
with her **hopes** and **dreams** pressed into her **journal.**
She is **me** and she is **you.**

Ella Soy Yo Y Ella Eres Tú

Huele a **salvia** y **aceite de lavanda.**
Sus **cristales** siempre están **cerca** dondequiera que vaya.
En sus **bolsillos**, en su **cartera**, en sus fundas de **almohada.**
Habla con sus **plantas** y **reza** cuando nadie la mira.
A veces es una **súplica.** A veces es **gratitud** y otras veces es para **ti.**
Practica **meditación** y otras noches enciende **velas.**
con sus **esperanzas** y **sueños** plasmados en su **diario.**
Ella soy **yo** y ella eres **tú.**

What do you need to **sage** away and **release**
to **make space** for what you wish?

Let It Go, Déjalo Ir

Enlightenment comes from
burning **sage,** or ***salvia,*** and
déjalo ir, as my ancestors say.
In this country, we say "**letting go**"
so the Universe can **guide** us like a lantern,
a flashlight or a ***velita***
into the portal of a **better *mañana***, or **tomorrow**.

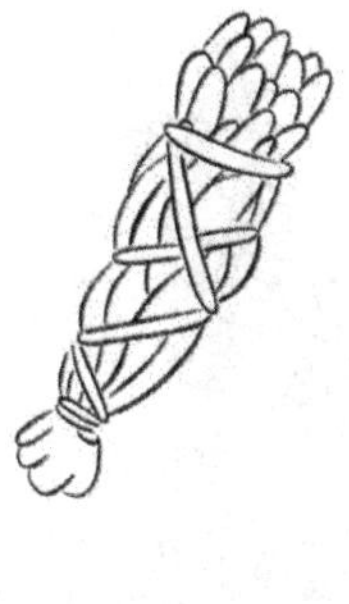

Transmuting

"When the world felt heavy for her, she **filled** a tiny
hand-made ceramic bowl with pieces of **sage**,
ignited it and let the clouds of smoke **rise**,
swirl and stretch its arms out like a dancer to **lift** off
what was weighing her down."

Transmutando

"Cuando el mundo le pesaba, **llenaba** un pequeño cuenco de cerámica hecho a mano con trozos de **salvia,** lo **encendía** y dejaba que las nubes de humo se **elevaran**, giraran y estiraran los brazos como una bailarina para **quitarse** lo que la pesaba."

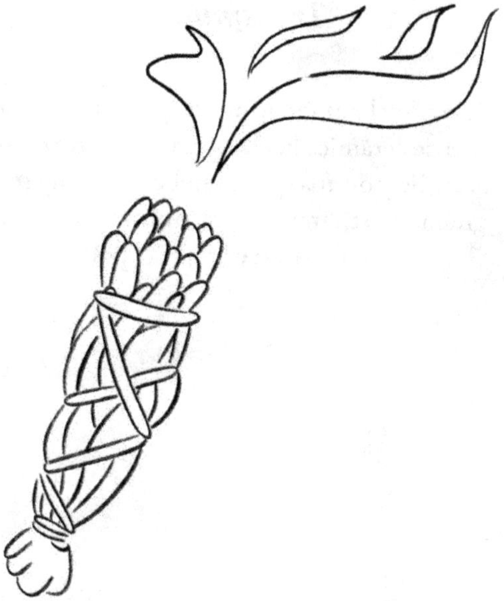

Sacred Smoke

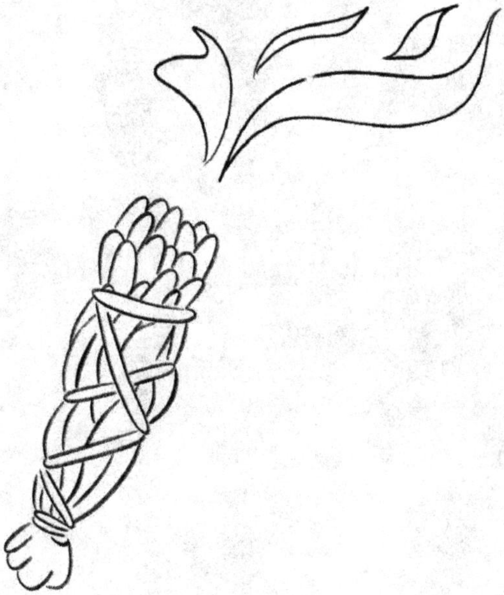

Sacred Smoke: Types And When To Use

Sage

Use: To purify heavy energy.
Best Time to Use: When things feel heavy, during or after being around a lot of energies, when you feel blocked and during a Full Moon.
Lunar Connection: Full Moon is the best time to use.

Palo Santo

Use: To lift your aura and restore positive energy.
Best Time to Use: When the energy feels good and you wish to magnify it.
Lunar Connection: New Moon is the ideal cycle to use.

Incense

Use: To enhance your meditation, yoga or another ritual practice.
Best Time to Use: When you need to feel centered and focused. It also helps to alleviate stress and creates a soothing energy.
Lunar Connection: Incense works with all moons.

Bay Leaf

Use: Manifesting.
Best Time to Use: Burn one to raise the positive vibration in your space. Take it up a level by writing down your intention on one and then burning it.
Lunar Connection: Bay leaves work with all moons.

Sacred Smoke: How To Properly Use

On a Loved One:

Have them close their eyes and think about what they desire to release as you sage them with intention. Tell them to envision it being released as you perform this ritual. Start at the top of their head and retrace their silhouette. Make sure they extend their arms out and have them lift the bottom of their feet when you get to that part of the body. Many people don't realize how we can pick up energy from the ground. Sage both their front and back side. Many people have energy lodged in their back from "backstabbers" or ***mal de ojo***, which is envy and jealousy. You might notice that a certain part of their body was holding more energy than others.

If you do, spend more time in that area.

[To seal the practice, have them choose a prayer intuitively from *My Little Prayer Book: 75 Prayers, Poems and Mantras for Illumination*. I recommend **Calling Back My Power** on Page 36 or **Etheric Cords** on Page 42.]

In Your Home:

Light the sage and move through every nook and cranny in your space. Retrace door frames, furniture, cabinets and closets. As you move through each part of your space, say: ***"I release energy that doesn't serve my beautiful home. I ask the Universe to take it now and I bless my space with sweet love, wonderful prosperity, incredible joy and excellent health."***

Then, open your windows or doors and allow the smoke to be released.

In Your Office Or Place Of Business:

Light the sage and move through **every nook and cranny** in your office or place of business. Retrace the **front door (inside and out)** and say: ***"Prosperity enters this door daily for my business now."*** Retrace any other **door frames, furniture, cabinets and closets**. As you move through each part of your office or place of business, say: ***"I release energy that doesn't serve my space, I ask the Universe to take it now and my business is now blessed with abundance."*** Then, open the windows or doors and allow the smoke to be released. If you work remotely, sage the items you use for work such as a computer, phone, notebook and pen. Perhaps you sell products, it is important you clear those items, too and thank them for being purchased.

In Your Car:

Once you have cleaned your car **inside and out**. It is lovely to sage your car and ask it to take you on many wonderful, fun joyous adventures, to big opportunities and anywhere you'd like to go. Say: ***"Thank you Universe for helping me arrive at the most beautiful moments, the right places and time for my successful career and to a life of love and travel."***

Traveling with Sage:

I recommend traveling with your sage. Keep it tucked in your **purse**. It doesn't have to be lit to work. It serves as a **protection**, too. If you stay in a **hotel**, sage the room for safe travel and rest. Maybe you are trying to book more **travel**, whip out the stick and sage the **inside and outside of your suitcase**. Inside, on a sheet of paper, write out: ***"Thank you Universe for the trips to X Y Z intention and as many details as possible."***

Purification

"Every morning **she rises** with a tangerine sun,
lights her sage to **purify** her mind, body and soul
and **bows** down to the most beautiful glowing goddess:
herself."

Purificación

"Cada mañana **se levanta** con un sol color mandarina,
enciende su salvia para **purificar** su mente, cuerpo y alma y
se **inclina** ante la diosa resplandeciente más bella:
ella misma."

Her Purse Essentials

Lip gloss, a sage stick, lavender oil,
a couple of crystals and her wallet.

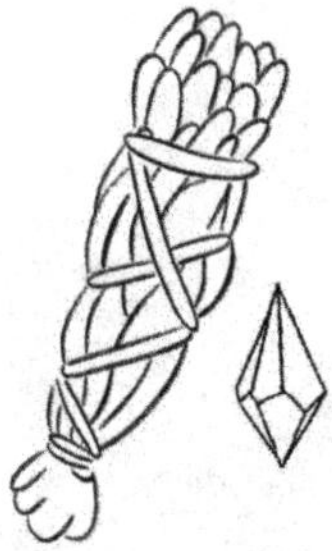

Lo Esencial De Su Cartera

Brillo de labios, una palo de salvia, aceite de lavanda,
un par de cristales y su billetera.

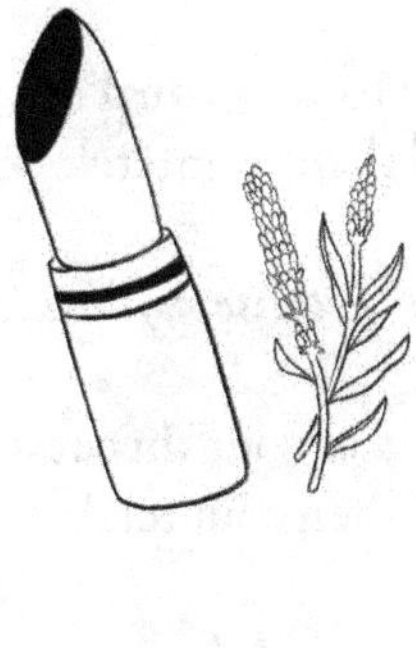

Sage Yourself Meditation

Saging yourself is a powerful tool to self-connect, relax and release. This beautiful meditation will help you get centered and grounded. It is great to use for the Full Moon.

Light your **sage.**

Close your **eyes** or cast them down.

Take a deep **breath** in and hold it 'til the count of 5. Then, exhale.

Open your **eyes.** Now, begin to **trace** your **silhouette**, chakra by chakra.

Start at the top of your **head** and move clockwise
and then counterclockwise.

Say: "***I welcome*** *downloads and* ***guidance*** *now.*"

Move the wand to your **third eye.** Move clockwise
and then counterclockwise.

Say: "***I ignite*** *my* ***intuition.***"

Place the wand at your **throat.** Move clockwise
and then counterclockwise.

Say: "*My* ***words*** *become my* ***reality.***"

Now, carry the wand to your **heart**. Move clockwise and then counterclockwise.

Say: "***I*** *live a life* ***full*** *of* ***love***."

Gently, place the wand by your **belly**. Move clockwise and then counterclockwise.

Say: "***Everything*** *is* ***solvable*** *through my limitless* ***power***."

Spark your **joy** by pointing the sage towards your **pelvic area**, moving it clockwise and then counterclockwise.

Say: "***I am a creative*** *genius and live a fulfilling life of joy and* ***pleasure***."

Lastly, **ground** yourself by taking the sage stick to your **legs** and the bottom of your **feet**. Move it up and down clockwise and counterclockwise.

Say: "*I am grounded, grateful and* ***trust*** *my* ***journey***."

Flow

"When I feel like my soul is screaming,
the **water** soothingly **whispers** that I will be fine.
'I will remind you how to **flow**.'"

Fluir

"Cuando siento que mi alma grita,
el **agua** me susurra **dulcemente** que estaré bien.
'Te recordaré cómo **fluir.**'"

A Woman's Power

A **woman** knows how to **heal** herself by
submerging in a **tub of water**, brimming with **flowers.**
Rose petals, marigolds, lavender:
the **cure** for tears, anger and fear.
Every time she scrubs a **soapy petal** to her skin,
it peels off **her** one by one.
And you doubt ***magic*** *exists?*

El Poder De Una Mujer

Una **mujer** sabe cómo **curarse** a sí misma
sumergiéndose en una **bañadera** llena de **flores**.
Pétalos de rosa, caléndulas, lavanda:
la **cura** para las lágrimas, la ira y el miedo.
Cada vez que se frota la piel con un **pétalo de jabón**,
se despega de **ella** uno por uno.
*¿Y dudas de que exista la **magia**?*

Shower Release Meditation

This is one of my favorite fast-working meditations to help soothe your soul and wash away what no longer serves you. You will walk out feeling refreshed, renewed and calm.

Instructions:

Light **sage** and place in a safe container.

Turn on the **shower.**

Step inside when the water feels like the **perfect temperature.**

Next, **close your eyes.**

Take a **deep breath in** and start to think about the **first thing** you'd like to **release** from your mind, body and spirit.

Then, **exhale** and feel the **water washing** away what no longer serves you.

Repeat.

Take a **deep breath in** and think about the **second thing** you'd like to **release** from your mind, body and spirit.

Then, **exhale** and feel the **water rinsing** off what feels heavy and transmuting it.

Last round. Take a **deep breath in** and think about the **third thing** you'd like to **release** from your mind, body and spirit.

Exhale and feel the **water cleansing** and restoring your **power back.**

Creating Sacred Spaces

Broom

The **broom** is the **magic wand** that also moves energy.
Why do you think **witches** fly with one?
If you wish to **fly**, grab your boom and clean.

Escoba

La **escoba** es la **varita mágica** que también mueve la energía.
¿Por qué tú crees que las **brujitas** vuelan con una?
Si quieres **volar**, empieza a limpiar.

How Cleaning Your Home Helps You Manifest

Cleaning your space is one of the quickest ways to **align** yourself and **make space** for your abundance to arrive. Why is this? Well, your space is a reflection of yourself. Too much **clutter** means the same is happening in your mind. Too much **disorganization** duplicates in your thoughts and actions. Mess and filth is low vibrational, leading to sadness, anger, bad health and even poverty. Let's bring **harmony** and **flow** into our spaces now.

Scan Your Space: Meticulously scan your space and see which area invigorates and which doesn't.

Remove Blocks: Open your **drawers**, rummage through them, **organize** and **donate** items you haven't used and toss out the rest. Place items in a donation bag and the rest in a garbage bag. You will feel the release instantaneously.

Better Health: Open your **kitchen cabinets, refrigerator and freezer. Organize** foods. **Toss out** unhealthy foods. **Stock** with **alive foods**. As the adages go, "you are what you eat" and "food is medicine." Therefore, the cleaner and more **conscious** you eat, the easier it is to reach your **health** goals. If you have serious goals, starting a **food diary** is necessary. Here, you can write down everything you eat so you can get a **better** grasp at what else you need to release and tweak.

Confidence: Go through your **clothing racks, shoes and accessories.** Notice which articles need to be donated and which can stay. If you haven't worn something in a long time like 3 months, it is time to toss it. You may have outgrown it or it no longer resonates with you. Giving an item to someone in need is **good karma**. You'll not only gain more confidence but you'll also get some extra blessings for a good deed. Remember to dress as you want the world to see you. It is important to **show up** as your **best** and **highest** self to receive daily **abundance**.

Clarity: Water is connected to **intuition, emotions and flow of prosperity**. You should enjoy showering or bathing, which opens your third eye and lets you get insight or a peek into the future. Making sure this personal space is clean and orderly. It should **smell good** and there should be an **element of fire** to balance out the water. Something like a metal bin, a candle or a red crystal like a garnet. Another lovely thing to have in your bathroom is a picture of some items in your **vision book, words of affirmation** or some **intentions.** Having it hung up there will inspire you daily.

Grounding: It is key to **sweep**, mop and make your floors sparkle. Go under the bed, **move furniture** and scoop up any hidden dust. Floors are **connected** to your root chakra which is about trust, grounding and having your basic needs met. Consider also bringing in some **houseplants** to help with grounding. [On page 320, I list my favorite houseplants and their benefits.]

Self-Love: Mirrors are connected to **self-love.** Clean your mirrors and attach beautiful **words of encouragement** to see each day. Maybe start a ritual of writing a **compliment** a day on a Post-It and sticking it on your mirror. Another helpful thing you can do is post a **future letter** to yourself to remind you to keep moving **forward.**

Romance: Go to the **bedroom.** Clean it. Make sure there are elements of fire in there. Some can be candles, red crystals like **Garnet** and metal furniture or accents. For plants think: **Anthurium**, or plants with heart-shaped leaves, like Pothos or Philodendron.
Remember no family photos here, mirrors or television.
The focus should be solely on **intimacy.**

Good Family and Friendships: The **living room** is a place to invite others to sit with you when they come over. Make it **welcoming.** Put soothing plants to bring **grounding.** One great recommendation is a bookshelf to share books and swap stories with **loved ones.**

My Space

"My **space** is a physical **reflection** of myself.
If I want to create **peace**, **love**, **prosperity** and **joy**,
I must **pour love** into my space first to help my goals **manifest** even more."

Mi Espacio

"Mi **espacio** es un **reflejo** físico de mí misma.
Si quiero crear **paz, amor, prosperidad** y **alegría,** primero debo **verter amor** en mi espacio para ayudar a que mis objetivos se **manifiesten** aún más."

Space Check-Off List for Abundance

Use this check off list during Full and New Moons to keep the energy flowing full of abundance and to help you feel your best.

Is my space **clean** and **organized**?

Does my space **smell good** and **feel welcoming**?

Is my **kitchen** organized and clean?

Is my **living room** wonderful and ready to host guests?

Is my **closet neat, color-coordinated** and is it **easy to find** to what I need?

Does my **bathroom** sparkle and feel **refreshed** for myself and guests?

Are my **cabinets** and **drawers tidy**?

Does the **refrigerator** and **freezer** house nourishing, delicious **healthy** foods?

Is my **laundry** done and put away?

Are my **dishes** clean and placed in their **proper area**?

Are my **windows** and **mirrors clean for clarity** and good self-love?

Is my **bed** made with **fragrant** sheets and is my bedroom **organized**?

Do I have gorgeous **flowers or plants** in my home for grounding?

Is there anything **broken or expired** to toss out?

Can I **donate items** I no longer use to receive **good karma**?

Are my **floors** clean?

Do the **light** fixtures work and the **plumbing**?

Is my **doorway** welcoming?

Do I have **Feng shui bells** on the door to transmute energy?

Do I have a **water fountain** near the entrance to cleanse the energy in my space daily and bring **prosperity** and flow?

Do I have **encouraging** words, books or other **elements** to fill my space so I stay inspired and full of faith?

Welcoming

"She placed a fresh bouquet of **sunflowers** in a vase, **organized** her shelves and cabinets, made her floors and countertops **sparkle** with a sprinkle of lavender oil and **blessed** her home with loving affirmations. There was a knock at her door a few days later. The **abundance** she had asked for had **arrived**."

Bienvenida

"Colocó un ramo fresco de **girasoles** en un jarrón, **organizó** sus estantes y gabinetes, hizo **brillar** sus pisos y mesetas con una pizca de aceite de lavanda y **bendijo** su hogar con afirmaciones amorosas. Unos días después, tocaron a su puerta. Había llegado la **abundancia** que había **pedido.**"

Cleaning Your Space For Good Vibes Meditation

Light a **candle** for guidance.
Say: "Universe, guide me and support me today."

Burn **incense** to purify your space.
Say: "I purify my mind, body and thoughts."

Put on some **music** that inspires you.
Say: "I am inspired and welcome positive vibrations."

Organize your space and toss out or put things away.
Say: "Everything is in order now to receive my abundance."

Put **laundry** to wash, and fold and hang clothes, sheets and towels.
Then, put everything in its proper place.
Say: "Thank you Universe for washing away my blocks and placing me in the right place to receive opportunities."

Scrub counter tops, shelves and tables.
Say: "My place holds lots of beautiful things."

Wash windows and mirrors.
Say: "Life is clear now. I can see what I need to do and the blessings in my life."

Broom and then mop your floors.
Say: "I am on the right path and it gets easier and easier to see it."

Bring in fresh flowers or plants.
Say: "My goals and dreams are blooming."

Open **windows** and burn **sage.**
Say: "I release whatever doesn't serve my mind, body and spirit and now welcome the best and highest version of me."

Traveling

"I am learning that **life** needs a '**carry-on**'
and not all this extra baggage."

Viajando

"Estoy aprendiendo que **la vida** necesita un '**equipo de mano**' y no todo este equipaje extra."

Unpacking List

We have all heard of packing lists for our travels. Well, today we are making an **unpacking list** for our journey here on Earth. More often than not, many of us tend to hold onto people, places, things, moments and past experiences that aren't aligned with our future selves anymore. **Not unpacking stalls our blessings and delays us from living our best life.**

Some examples of blocks to unpack are:

A behavior
Your comfort zone
Your current home
A low vibrating emotion
A habit
A job
A lifestyle
A limiting belief
Fear of failure
Fear of the unknown
Someone from your inner circle
A past experience
A relationship
Scarcity mindset
Societal or cultural conditioning

Unpacking List Check-Off

I am **unpacking** this **behavior:**

I am **unpacking** this **limiting belief:**

I am **unpacking** this **habit:**

I am **unpacking** this **conditioning:**

I am **unpacking** this **unhealthy relationship:**

I am **unpacking** this **scarcity mindset:**

I am **unpacking** this **past experience:**

I am **unpacking** this **fear:**

I am **unpacking** this **frustration:**

I am **unpacking** this **anger:**

I am **unpacking** this **sadness:**

I am **unpacking** this **memory:**

Spiritual Scissors

I had to learn to take my **spiritual scissors**
and mercilessly **cut off the cords** that held me hostage
from **the person I wanted to be.**

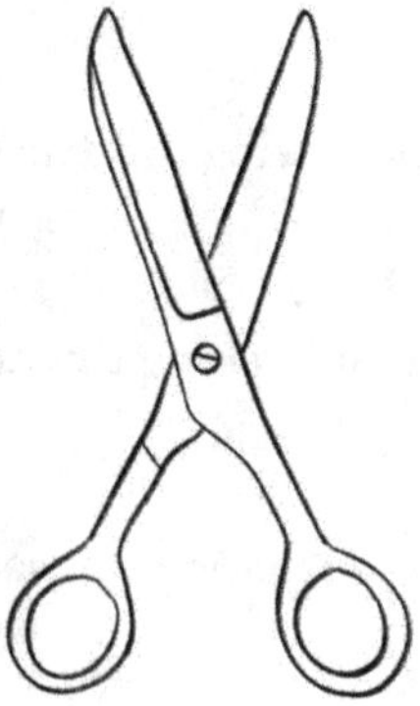

Tijeras Espirituales

Tuve que aprender a tomar mis **tijeras espirituales**
y **cortar las cuerdas** que me mantenían como rehén
de **la persona que quería ser.**

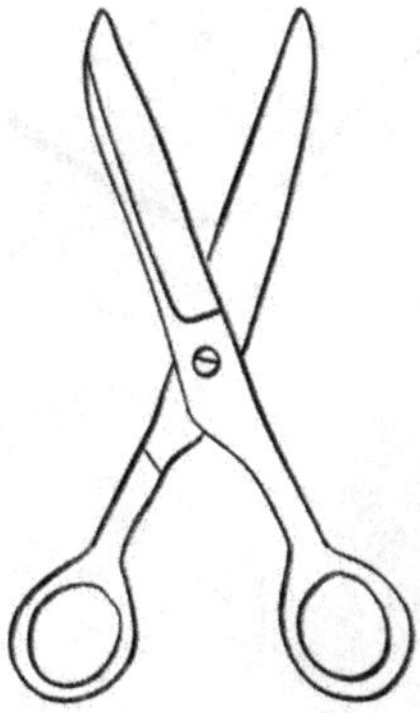

Sacred Self-Love

Soulmate

"**You** are one of your **greatest soulmates.**
Learn to **love** all the parts of **you.**"

Alma Gemela

"Eres una de tus **mejores almas gemelas.**
Aprende a **amar** todas tus partes."

My Forever Love

We sometimes forget that the **person** we are
in a **forever committed** relationship is **ourselves**
and we owe ourselves all the
love, compassion, **respect**, patience and **joy**.
It is only when **we love ourselves** the right way,
that **we** can **attract** others that can **love us** this **deep**.

Mi Amor Por Siempre

A veces olvidamos que la **persona** que estamos
en una **relación comprometida** para siempre
somos **nosotras** mismas y nos debemos todo el
amor, la compasión, el **respeto**, la paciencia y la **alegría.**
Sólo cuando **nos amamos a nosotras mismas** de la manera correcta,
podemos **atraer** a otros que **puedan amarnos** tan **profundamente.**

Why I've Never Married

When they ask me why I've never **married,**
I shrug, **pretending** not to know why.

I don't tell them about the **black eye** and the
bruises that once dotted my arms and legs.

How **darkness swallowed** me into the pits of its
belly like a **whale** before I crawled out.

I politely listen to them make **suggestions**
of how to meet someone without **confessing**
I grew **barbed wire** around my **heart.**

That's what happens to women when men use
their hands try to break our **bodies.**

We turn into **roses** that will make you bleed if
you reach for **us.**

Sometimes, these women throw **daggers** at me,
like, "You're picky, you're not getting any younger,
you have bad luck, and you should give some
guys a **chance.**"

I keep **quiet** about the night the cops
found me **strewn** out like garbage
on the side of the street one October
evening for not being "**picky**" enough.

Fingermarks **indented** around my neck.
Lips **swollen** like starfruit.
Hands **peppered** with gravel and ribbons of
blood **streaming** out of me
for giving some guy too many "**chances.**"

"Don't you want someone to **love**?" they press.

I become as still as a **forest**,

remembering how many **waterfalls** I'd make
before I could say those **words** to myself.

"I **love** myself."

Healthy Love

Healthy love begins with the self.
What you **seek** you must first **give to yourself.**
Once you do that, you can attract the right person into your life.

Take yourself out, buy yourself **flowers**, treat yourself to special **moments**,
connect with your **feelings** and **set boundaries.**

When it comes to **pain**,
your pain can be **alchemized** into your greatest **power**.
Be gentle and compassionate with your soul as you heal.
Never be ashamed of your mistakes or your past.
It **taught you** something you had to **learn**,
and now, you have your present self to create your dream future.

Make a **list** of what you **seek** in a **relationship**,
and then make a list of what you bring to the table.

Mirrors, Espejos

The people around you are ***espejos,*** or **mirrors,**
reflecting, or ***reflejando,*** your own
Cosmos,
tu pasado, tu presente y tu futuro,
your **past, present and future**,
all existing simultaneously.
To the old **versions** of you that once existed in the Milky Way,
send them ***amor*** and move forward.
She did the **best** she could with the **knowledge** she had.
To **present you**, get out of your comfort zone, **take chances**,
strengthen your faith and find **one thing** to be **grateful** for every day.
Whether it is a **topaz sky**, laughter with **friends**, or a **date** with yourself.
Acknowledge it so it can **multiply** in other forms of **abundance**.
To **future you**, envision her.
Make a **list** of what she is like and her **life**.
Step into **her** as if you were walking through one **door** and into another.

Who are you most **like** and **why**?

Where have you **grown**?

Who is someone that **inspires** you to grow?

What are some **attributes** you **admire** in someone
that you wish for your future self to **blossom** into?

Who is **someone** that reflects an **old version** of you
that you need to hold with more **compassion**?

Is there anyone you need to **let go** of or **distance** yourself from
because they refuse to grow?

Who is someone that is **growing simultaneously** with you
on the journey right now?

When **you** look in the mirror at yourself,
what are some **beautiful** things you see about **yourself**?

What are some **changes** you'd like to make
so you can live a **happier, healthier and peaceful life**?

Remember we cannot change people, we can only change ourselves to get the results we wish for. What can you **commit** to now to **change** for you?

Boundaries

"When you create **boundaries,**
you become a **temple of self-love.**"

Límites

"Cuando creas **límites,**
te conviertes en un **templo del amor propio.**"

Espinas Of Self-Love

I grew **thorns** down my spine to
protect me from men like you who just
wanted to take my **petals**
and not water me with **real love.**
I was born a ***flor***.
I was Peony, Rosa, Girsasol.
I was **Petunia, Daisy and Gardenia.**
But I grew ***espinas* of self-love**;
tiny **blades** because you couldn't respect
my **boundaries.**
Now, you would **learn** how much it hurts
to reach for **someone** and bleed.

Espinas Del Amor Propio

Me crecieron **espinas** por la columna para
protégeme de hombres como tú que simplemente
quería tomar mis **pétalos**
y no regarme con **amor verdadero.**
Nací **flor.**
Yo era Peonía, Rosa, Girsasol.
Yo era **Petunia, Daisy y Gardenia.**
Pero me crecieron **espinas de amor propio**;
cuchillas diminutas porque no podías respetar
mis **límites.**
Ahora, entenderás cuánto duele
alcanzar a **alguien** y sangrar.

Teacher

"**Slow down, sit** with yourself and **listen**
to what your **spirit** needs to tell you.
The true **teacher** and **healer** lies within.
The **answers** and **guidance** are all inside you."

Maestra

"**Reduce la velocidad, siéntate** contigo misma y **escucha**
lo que tu **espíritu** necesita decirte.
La verdadera **maestra** y **curadora** está dentro.
Las **respuestas** y la **guía** están dentro de ti."

Muse

"True love begins with **being your own muse.**
Getting to know your true **self.**
What simple pleasures **ignite your soul.**
What your **goals** and **priorities** are before anyone else."

Musa

"El verdadero amor comienza **siendo tu propia musa.**
Conociendo tu verdadero **yo.**
Qué placeres simples **encienden tu alma.**
Cuáles son tus **objetivos** y **prioridades** antes que nadie."

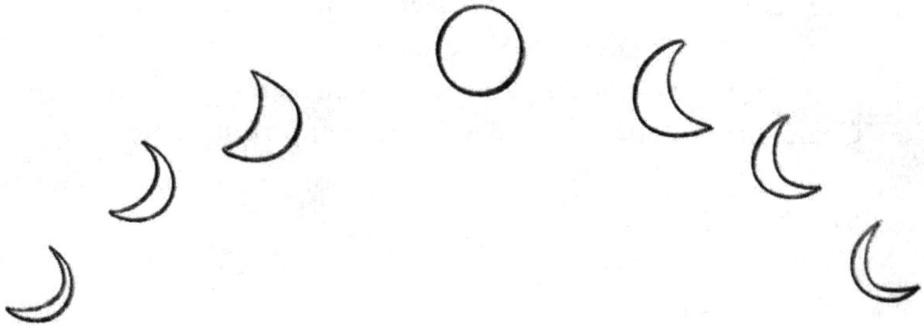

Cosmic Shifts

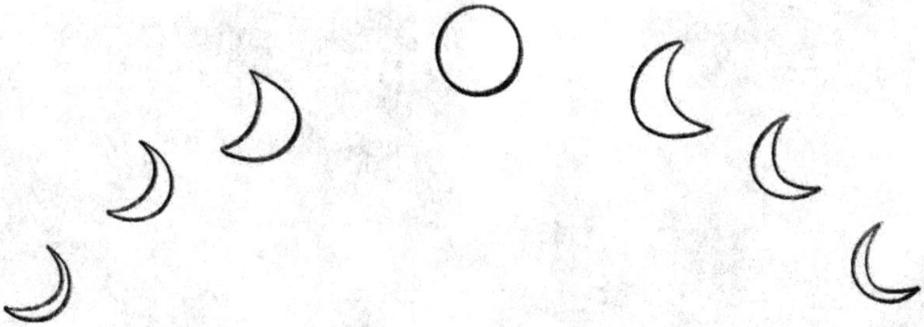

Mercury Retrograde

Mercury Retrograde is one of the few events that happens 3 to 4 times a year that is **beneficial** in helping you **grow** and **expand** fast. It is known as the **great review period.** It brings forth goals, relationships of all kinds and experiences that need to be **re-examined.**

Mercury Retrograde Guide

Speak slower, softer and clear to **avoid miscommunication.**

Re-read contracts and **proofread** documents.

Be aware that **exes** come back during this time.

Create boundaries for yourself and others.

Expect delays for protection.

Cancellations can happen for something better to come along.

Socialize with loving and kind people.

Deepen the connection with your heart
and what your **present** self needs to give your **future** self.

Avoid serious **surgeries** if you can.

Back up **technology**.

Make space for **magic** to happen.
Beautiful things happen during this time.

Lots of **wisdom** will come through.

Beautify your **space** and spend time **outside** to clean your **aura.**

New friendships form and old ones that are
meant to be in your life are **renewed.**

Burn bridges that lead nowhere.

Travel with an **extra 10 minutes** to avoid slow downs.

Stay grounded.

Be aware that this is a good time for **planning.**

Practice **daily affirmations** to stay mindful.

Make a list of how your **present self** is showing up for your **future self.**

Restart an **old project** that's been calling you.

Pay attention to **cycles** you need to **close** and
the people and things you need to let go of.

This is an excellent time for **self-reflection**, journaling
and working on your vision book.

Spend **quality time** with people you love and care about.

Because this is a **transformative time**,
ask yourself where you need a transformation.

Metamorphosis

"If you are ready for a **transformation,**
begin to make **small changes** every day until, one day,
the **big change** you've been praying for **arrives.**"

Metamorfosis

"Si estás lista para una **transformación,**
comienza a hacer **pequeños cambios** todos los días hasta que, un día,
llegue el **gran cambio** por el que has estado orando."

Eclipse Of The Heart Chakra

Just like Mercury Retrograde, **eclipses** bring about **rapid transformations.** They can happen up to five times a year. They are one of the many ways the Universe helps you let go of what is not aligned with **future you** and your **heart chakra.** There are two types of eclipses that happen. One is a **Solar Eclipse**, which takes place during a **New Moon.** The other is a **Lunar Eclipse**, which occurs simultaneously with a **Full Moon.**

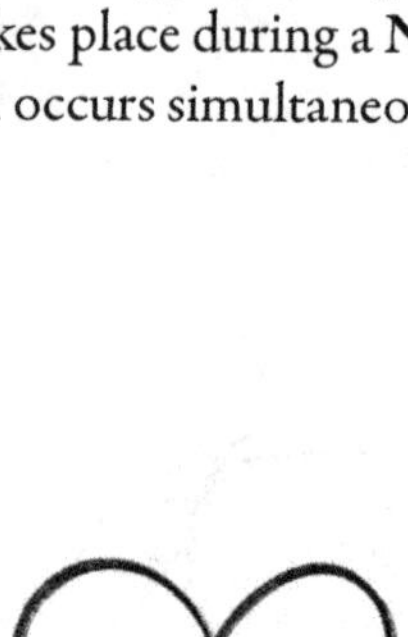

Eclipse Guide

Fast uncontrollable energy of **transformation**.

Brings **closure** and change.

Certain people and things will be **eclipsed** out that aren't in your future.

Gives a glimpse of what is coming in the **future** for you.

Opportunities come in droves. More than we can imagine.

A good time to **reflect** on what you want eclipsed out
and what blessing you'd like instead.

What **actions** are you **taking** now to step into the **future**?

What **actions** do you wish to take but need **help** from the **Universe** on?

Magic

"I make **space** for **magic** to arrive."

Magia

"Hago **espacio** para que llegue la **magia.**"

Learn To Walk Away

Learn to **walk away** from people and things
that no longer serve your **highest** and **best self**.
When in doubt, **ask** yourself,
Does this person leave me feeling ***peaceful*** *or* ***drained****?*
Goodbyes are not easy, but neither is repeating
a **cycle** over and over.

Aprenda A Alejarse

Aprende a **alejarte** de las personas y las cosas
que ya no sirven tú **mejor** y **más elevada** ser.
En caso de duda, **pregúntate**:
*¿Esta persona me deja en **paz** o **agotada**?*
Las **despedidas** no son fáciles, pero repetir
un **ciclo** tampoco.

My Hips Cast Love Spells

My ***caderas*** can cast **love spells** so
I'm **dancing** in the **moonlight** tonight,
shaking you off with my **hips**,
twirling you out of my **mind**,
singing you out of my **heart**,
because you don't **deserve**
a **place** there anymore.

I'm a **magnet** for **miracles**
on this Full Moon and
I **release** you and **manifest** someone just right
with a **snap** of my **finger**,
a **wink** of an **eye**,
a **sultry** hair **toss.**
He's about to arrive.

Beneath a **luminous lemon**-tinted sky,
my **intention**, like a fully-charged **crystal**,
activates my **words** into a **powerful spell**,
bringing **future** flash visions to me.

I'm **dancing** in the **moonlight** tonight.
A final **ritual.**

A wave **goodbye** to you,
and kiss **hello** to him:
my **half**,
my **flame**,
my **karmic blessing.**
My **third eye** already knows his name.

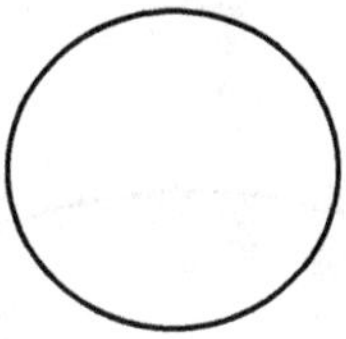

"Every ***adios*** leads you to a new ***hola***."

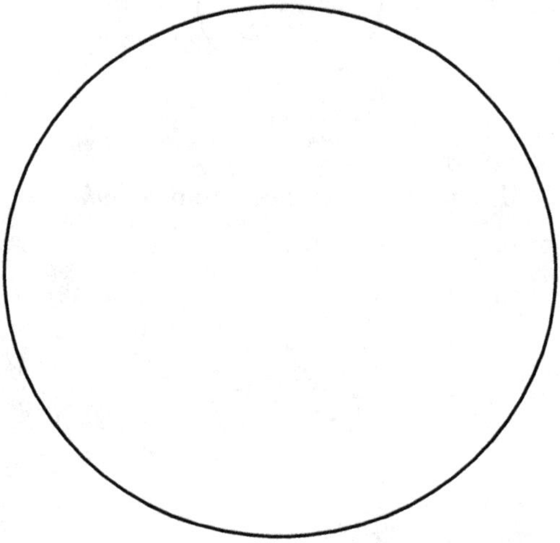

Full Moons

Why Full Moons Are Important

The Full Moon happens once a month, sometimes twice. It is a graduation period where we reflect on our life and notice what we need to let go of to make space for what we desire. It is connected to the first goddess who is learning to navigate life. Sage is also the sacred smoke we use on Full Moons to release.

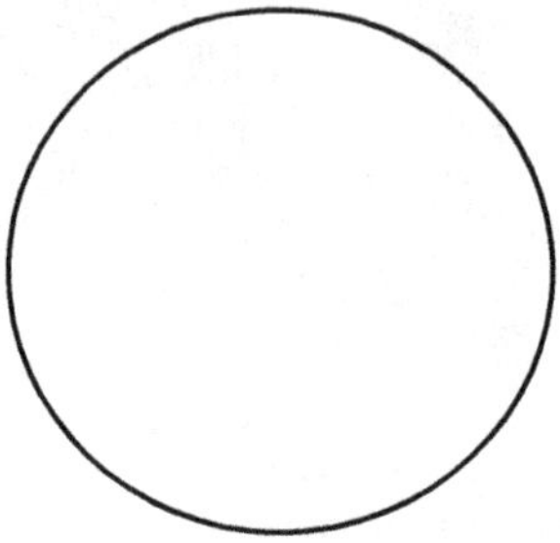

Full Moon Intentions

The Full Moon is a graduation period and a moment to reflect on where we are on the journey. It's insightful to look back at the last 30 days and notice our lessons and blessings. We can use this information to help us make better decisions about our future.

Directions: Set some Full Moon intentions below using the example as guidance.

Full Moon Intention Example:
My intention is: To create an amazing second book that is better than my first book.
3 details or more about it are: It is a self-help book, interactive, beautiful cover, best-seller and a reader favorite.
The block I am releasing: Anxiety of fast deadlines.
An action I am taking to manifest it is: Write daily, avoid distractions, meditate for enlightenment on what to include, exercise, eat healthy and sleep to do my best work.
Date: 4/11/24

My intention is:

3 details or more about it are:

The block I am releasing:

An action I am taking to manifest it is:

Date:

My intention is:

3 details or more about it are:

The block I am releasing:

An action I am taking to manifest it is:

Date:

My intention is:

3 details or more about it are:

The block I am releasing:

An action I am taking to manifest it is:

Date:

My intention is:

3 details or more about it are:

The block I am releasing:

An action I am taking to manifest it is:

Date:

My intention is:

3 details or more about it are:

The block I am releasing:

An action I am taking to manifest it is:

Date:

My intention is:

3 details or more about it are:

The block I am releasing:

An action I am taking to manifest it is:

Date:

My intention is:

3 details or more about it are:

The block I am releasing:

An action I am taking to manifest it is:

Date:

My intention is:

3 details or more about it are:

The block I am releasing:

An action I am taking to manifest it is:

Date:

My intention is:

3 details or more about it are:

The block I am releasing:

An action I am taking to manifest it is:

Date:

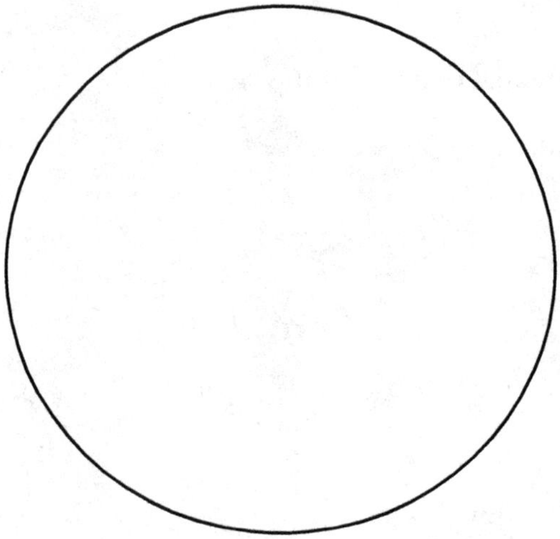

How Full Moons Can Help You

Full Moons can help you let go of what feels heavy in your mind, body and soul. In fact, there are many different types of Full Moons we experience throughout the year.

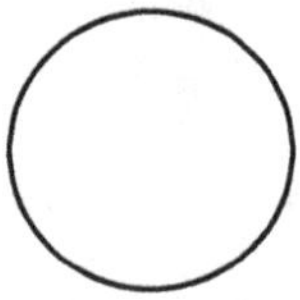

The 12 Full Moons

January: Wolf Moon
Meaning: Coined after hungry wolves howling.

February: Snow Moon
Meaning: Represents the abundance of snow falling.

March: Worm Moon
Meaning: It is the time when the soil starts warming up and earthworms start peeking out.

April: Pink Moon
Meaning: Derived from countless pink flowers blooming.

May: Flower Moon
Meaning: Connected to all the flowers blooming.

June: Strawberry Moon
Meaning: It pays homage to when strawberries are the most ripe.

July: Buck Moon
Meaning: It is when antlers grow on bucks.

August: Sturgeon Moon
Meaning: The fish during this period are found in large numbers.

September: Corn Moon
Meaning: Native Americans are harvesting their corn this month.

October: Hunter Moon
Meaning: Traditionally, this is when hunting took place to prepare for winter.

November: Beaver Moon
Meaning: This is usually when the little creatures are seen preparing for winter.

December: Cold Moon
Meaning: A beautiful moon that signifies the beginning of winter.

Other Special Moons

Blue Moon:
Happens every two and a half years.

Harvest Moon:
It is the Full Moon that is closest to Fall Equinox.

Full Moons + The Four Elements

Aside from the different names, each **Full Moon** highlights each month. Full Moons are connected to the **4 elements** (earth, water, fire and air). The elements help us experience **different energies** that assist us in **manifesting**. It is also encouraged to incorporate the element of the Full Moon in a ritual.

Earth Elements of The Full Moon

♉

Taurus:
Reminds you to treat yourself, always say the truth and beautify your home.

♍

Virgo:
Motivates you to organize, think logically and practice patience.

♑

Capricorn:
Encourages you to be more ambitious, strategic and disciplined.

Ritual Recommendations:
Burn **sage.**
Set an intention on a **bay leaf.**
Forest bathing.
Earthing (take off shoes and walk on grass).
Gardening.
Get a **pedicure.**
Go for a nice **Full Moon walk.**
Make a **Crystal Grid.**
Plant an **intention inside a plant.**

Water Elements of The Full Moon

♋

Cancer:
Increases your intuition, nudges you to listen to your feelings and play with art.

♏

Scorpio:
Helps you become more confident, resourceful and face your shadows.

♓

Pisces:
Inspires you to dream your intentions into existence, use your imagination to resolve and flow.

Ritual Recommendations:
Clean your windows for more clarity.
Do a **salt scrub** to cleanse your aura.
Clean **crystals in running water** or salt water (except for selenite).
Go for a **swim.**
Dip your **toes in the water.**
Walk in the rain.
Water your plants.
Journal next to running water to open up the channels of communication.
Boil cinnamon for abundance.

Fire Elements of The Full Moon

♈

Aries:
Ignites your passion, boosts your confidence
and helps you stay determined.

♌

Leo:
Influences you to step into your power,
helps you see your true talents and stay warm hearted.

♐

Sagittarius:
Opens you up to be more adventurous, playful and optimistic.

Ritual Recommendations:
Light a candle and recite intentions.
Write a **burn letter**, filling it up with everything you want to let go of and then burning it in a safe space.
Sage every nook and cranny of your space, prized possessions and loved ones.
Candle gazing.
Burn incense to help you focus on incoming messages from your divine team.
Spend time **meditating** in the sunshine.
Lay down in the sunshine and expose your belly to **activate your solar plexus** where your fire energy lies.

Air Elements of The Full Moon

♊

Gemini:
Shows you how to use your charm, be more social and adaptable.

♎

Libra:
Teaches you how to create more balance, fairness and romance.

♒

Aquarius:
Inspires to think out of the box and stand for the good of all.

Ritual Recommendations:
Open your windows and **air out old stagnant energy.**
Open doors. **Blow a pinch of cinnamon** out from the palm of your hand to welcome in abundance.
Savor outdoor breezes and cool air against your cheeks.
Do **breathwork.**
Revisit your **vision book** and tweak it to receive future messages.
Pull cards to get messages from the divine.

Full Moon Symptoms

Vivid dreams

Nervousness

Emotional and increased sensitivity

Great revelations

Irritation and anger

Insomnia

Fatigue

Heightened intuition

Faster manifesting

Full Moon Check-Off List

Use this list to work with the energy of the Full Moon three days before it happens or three days after. Choose whatever ritual calls to you.

Clean and organize to create harmony and open your space to receive the abundance you desire.

Use sacred smoke or essential oils to refresh.

Light a candle and set intentions [See page 97 for more on this].

Full Moon Intention: "*I release X energy and I replace it with X abundance.*"

Journal what has changed from the last Full Moon to now.

Make a 3-column list that includes the lessons you learned, what you're grateful for and the abundance that you received.

Work with the element the moon is in.

Meditate and pray. Use *My Little Prayer Book: 75 Prayers, Poems and Mantras for Illumination Full Moon Prayer* to dive deeper into prayer and meditation.

Make Full Moon water. Place a jar or bowl outside or by a windowsill filled with water at night. Then, on the following day, sprinkle around your space and on yourself to refresh the energy.

Work on your Vision Book. Add and tweak your vision for the year.

Get guidance. Ask a question and pull some cards.

Set crystals to charge outside or by a windowsill.

Bay Leaf Ritual

Make wishes on **bay leaves.**
Tattoo your intentions in black ink
against the green skin.
Strike a **match.**
Let the Universe **burn** away your **blocks**
and **transmute** your dreams into reality.

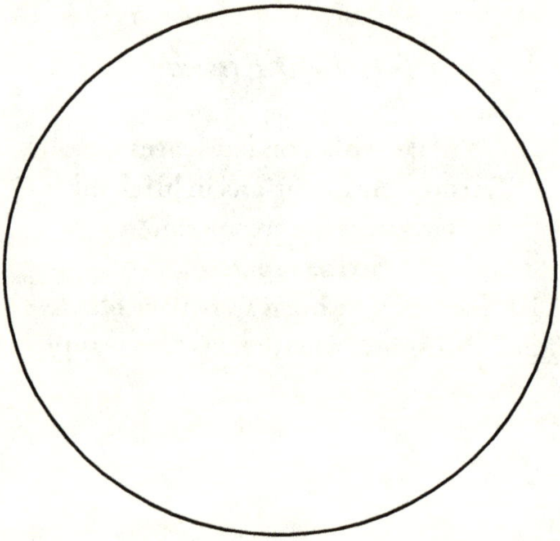

Full Moon Meditation

Light a candle for **guidance.**
Say: "Universe, I am ready to release what no longer serves me."

Burn incense or sage to **purify** your space.
Say: "I let go of what holds me back from being my best and highest self."

Write some intentions you'd like to experience in the next cycle.
Say: "I am ready to receive these intentions and be guided to them."

Journal about the last 30 days. What were your peaks and pits?
Say: "I am grateful for my last 30 day journey.
I know the best is yet to come."

Place one hand on the **heart** and the other on your **belly.**
Take three **inhales** and **exhales.**
Say: "I am blessed and good things happen for me."

Keep one hand on **heart** and the other on your **belly.**
Say: "I have limitless power to create my intentions."

Stay with one hand on **heart** and the other on your **belly.**
Say: "I am fully supported by my angels and ancestors."

Continue in the **same position.**
Say: "I know my intentions are manifesting right now."

Read your intentions.
Say: "Thank you Universe for helping me co-create these intentions."

Go **outside** and **howl at the moon** for fun.

Rebirth

"A **woman** who **cuts** her hair intentionally is performing a **rebirth** ritual with the divine."

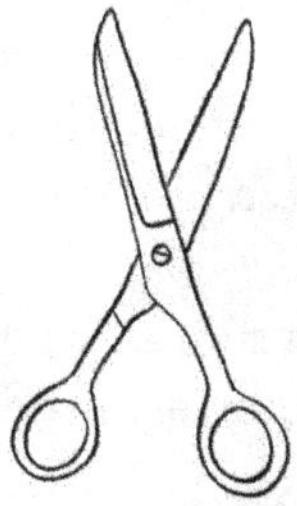

Renacimiento

"Una **mujer** que se **corta** el pelo intencionalmente está realizando un ritual de **renacimiento** con lo divino."

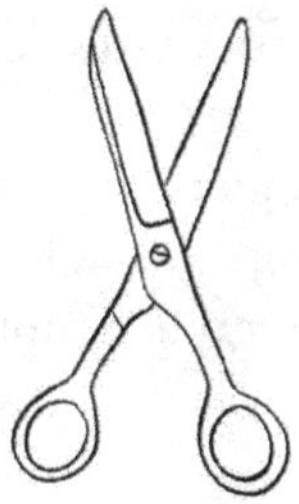

The Sacred Act Of A Haircut

A woman who **cuts** her **hair**
is performing a **rebirth ritual** with the divine.

She's partaking in a **moving prayer**
by **surrendering** and **severing**
all the **weight** of
old **stories** and pain
deeply woven within her **strands** and **heart.**

That's why you will see many of us
making rain with our eyes
as blades shear off our **locks**
and we witness the **funeral**
of our **old self.**

Letting go of who we were
and being **brave enough** to start over
is a **sacred act** that honors the soul.

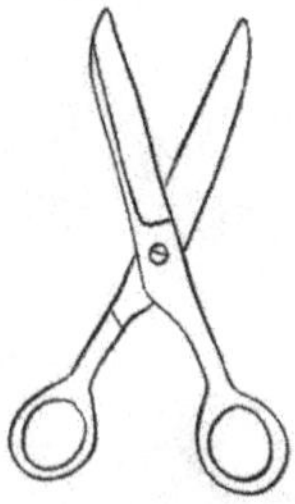

Best Times For A Haircut

The changing of the seasons:
Spring Equinox
Summer Solstice
Fall Equinox
Winter Solstice

Full Moons.

End of the year.

End of something significant.

Whenever your crown chakra calls for it.

To release energy.

When you're ready for a new beginning.

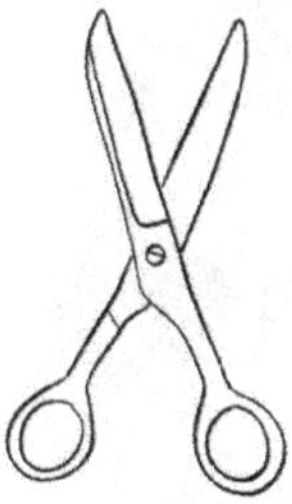

Wishes

"On Full Moons, she casts
prayers that **pierce** the sky
like tiny rocket ships with **wishes.**"

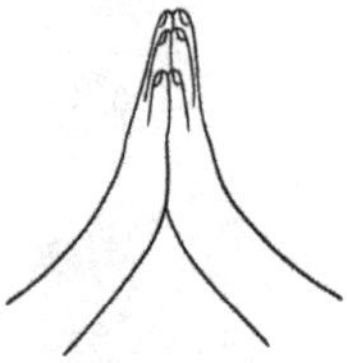

Deseos

"En las lunas llenas, ella lanza
oraciones que **perforan** el cielo
como pequeños cohetes con **deseos.**"

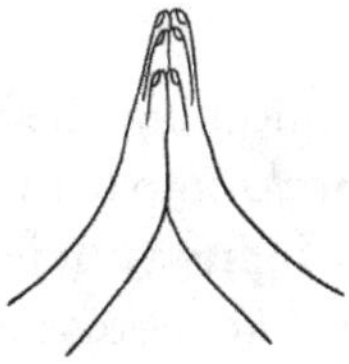

When She Becomes Loba, Wolf

A **woman** with a broken heart
is just a wolf
remembering her **wild** again.

On Full Moons, she casts
prayers that **pierce** the sky
like tiny rocket ships with **wishes.**
And she **releases** glorious heart-filled howls
that sometimes **echo** back to her
Aaaaaooouuu aaaaoouu aaaooouu
between the **buzzing** of
cicadas and crickets.
She **becomes** part of a pack
with distant neighbors on balconies
and porches **howling** with her.

A woman with a broken heart
is just a wolf **learning** how
how to claw her
way back to **herself.**

Early mornings, before
the sun **peeks** into her window,
she **lights** a candle
and **sits** like a lotus flower,
rising, blooming, **strengthening**,
summoning back her **power**
from anything
or anyone who stole it from her.

A woman with a broken heart
tattoos the words along her
ribcage so she never forgets
what pain feels like when you
put **yourself** second instead of first.

A woman with a mended heart
is clearly a wolf **looking** in the mirror,
painting a pretty red pout
that she slowly lifts like curtain
to **reveal** a dazzling fang-toothed smile.
Aaaaoooau

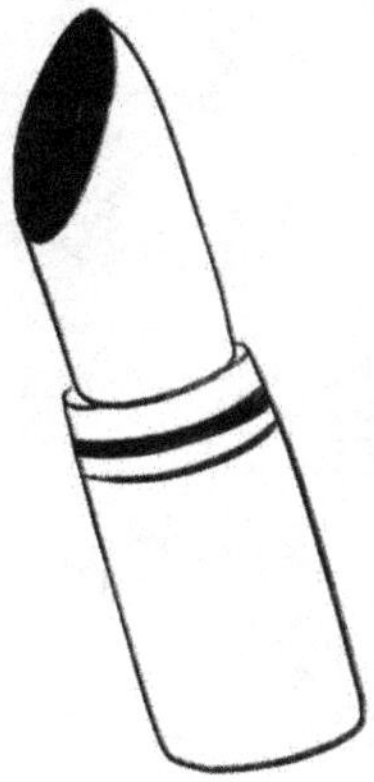

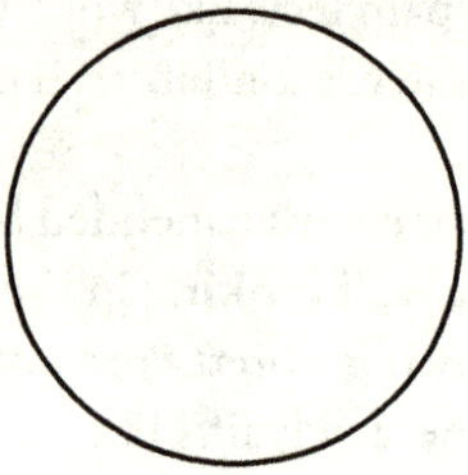

"The Full **Moon** is your **graduation** period."

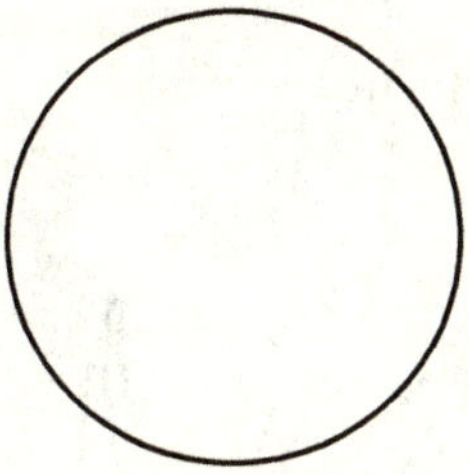

"La **luna** llena es tu período de **graduación.**"

Lavender Oil, Aceite de Lavanda

Lavender has a calming effect. This chapter shows you how to find your own lavender oil at any time to reach inner peace. We connect with the New Moon in this section.

Bloom

"When I **surrender** and **trust** that it's all working out,
fields of **lavender bloom** around me."

Florecer

"Cuando me **rindo** y **confío** en que todo está funcionando, campos de **lavanda florecen** a mi alrededor."

What do I need to **trust** is **working** out for me right now?

How can I be more **intentional** in my life?

Intention

"The more I live **intentionally**, the more life unfolds like a bouquet of **lavender flowers** for me."

Intención

"Cuando vivo más **intencional**, más se desarrolla
la vida para mí como un ramo de **flores de lavanda.**"

Perfume

"She dabbed the **lavender oil** behind her ears,
her wrists and on the nape of her neck.
That was her signature scent."

Perfumar

"Ella se aplicó el **aceite de lavanda** detrás de las orejas,
las muñecas y atrás del cuello.
Ese era su perfume característico."

The Elixir Of Lavender Oil And Violetas

She dabbed the **lavender oil** behind her ears, her wrists and on the nape of her neck. That was her **signature scent**. That and ***Violetas***. The perfume every Cuban baby is doused with after a bath. As an adult she still wore it because it reminded her of simple joys like being at her tia-abuelas and running in the golden sunshine with her hair still wet after a bath. She would air dry it, waiting for the ***cocuyos,*** or **fireflies**, to appear. These beautiful creatures were like little stars dancing in her hands and in the night sky. Even to this day, they leave her awestruck.

She toted lavender oil in her purse because it made her **calm**. It was the **elixir** that made the giant waves that thrashed inside her from time to time **soften into stillness**. It was her weapon in a world where her ancestors and even her parents were forced to leave everything behind to cross oceans in search of freedom.

Her little ears listened to the word **liberty** but it would take some years before she truly understood what ***libertad*** meant and the sacrifices her familia made.

She was born in *tierra,* or soil, that allowed her to be a ***bocana,*** or a **loud mouth**, from an early age. This often led to her getting her teeth scrubbed with a bar of soap until her eyes leaked steamy tears. And even here where she could yell guttural screams for her ancestors in America. She wasn't fully welcomed. She was "too *blanca,* or white," according to some of the Spanish kids and "too Cuban" to be fully accepted by some of the gringo kids. What did they call her? "White-tina." **What did she know with her milky, *leche*, skin about being Latina?**

It wasn't only her. She saw it happen to her mother, too. Usually, when they'd walk into a Cuban restaurant to get food similar to the one her *Abuela* spent hours in the *cocina* making.

Words that bit and stung. "Why were these *Gringo-Americanos* coming here?" the staff and restaurant-goers would mutter. Her mother, with all her **sweet-guava-kindness**, patiently waited and eventually got their attention after they bumped several people in line in front of her.

When it was finally her mother's turn, the Spanish came out of her mouth, leaving their annoyed, ignorant faces frozen with a look of shock.

By the time she reached her mother's age not much had changed in the world. Colorism still existed in her culture. Unlike her mom, her spirit was a little more like ***vinagre y sal***, or **salt and vinegar**. She wanted to be sweet like **flan**, or ***dulce de coco***—and she was most of the time. Except for moments when the giant waves rose inside and thrashed within her body. And those waves she knew weren't just hers, but generations of ancestors' stories rising within. This is why she used ***aceite de lavanda***, or **lavender oil**.

Balance

"In Spanish, we call the moon ***La Luna*** because she is our **feminine essence.** We call the sun ***El Sol,*** as he represents our **masculine energy**."

La Luna Y El Sol

You are the **moon** and the **sun**.
You have always been meant to **shine**
in the **dark** and in the **light**.

I am the **moon** and the **sun**.
I have always been meant to **shine**
in the **dark** and in the **light**.

Soy la ***luna*** *y el* ***sol.***
Siempre he estado destinada a ***brillar***
en la ***oscuridad*** *y en la* ***luz.***

Shine

"I am the **moon**, the **sun** and I was **born to shine**."

Brillar

"Soy la **luna,** el **sol** y **nací para brillar.**"

Yin

The **moon** is **Yin.**
It is **feminine.**
It is reflective. It gently **plans.**
It is **quiet, creative** and **soft.**
It is connected with the **night sky.**
Fall and **winter** embody this energy.
It is **cozy,** self-caring and **contemplating.**
Yin is my **intention,** my **wish,** my **goal.**
Holding my **palms up** to my lips like I am about to
blow **confetti** into the air, I speak my **dreams**
to **existence.**

Yang

The sun is **Yang** energy.
It is **masculine.**
It is **impulsive.** It takes **action.**
It evokes the **spiritual warrior** within.
It is **fire** moving **fast like a cheetah** or **a stallion galloping.**
It is **outgoing like an actor** on stage and **clear like a Bahamian ocean.**
It is **assertive** and **connected** to the light.
Spring and **summer** do cartwheels in this energy and remind me
to step out of my **comfort zone** and put **action** into my words.

Yin Qualities

Ease
Feminine
Intuitive
Introverted
Nurturing
Passive
Patience
Quiet
Receptive
Relaxed
Sensitive
Softness
Thoughtful
Visionary

Yang Qualities

Active
Adventurous
Assertive
Courageous
Emotional
Excitement
Flexible
Extroverted
Impulsive
Masculine
Power
Social
Strong

Yin Yang Venn Diagram

Fill in the venn diagram with your
Yin qualities on one side and your **Yang** qualities on the other.
Let's create balance.

Zodiacs With Yin And Yang Energy

Zodiacs with Yin energy are water and earth signs:

Cancer
Capricorn
Pisces
Scorpio
Taurus
Virgo

Zodiacs with Yang energy are air and fire signs:

Aries
Aquarius
Gemini
Leo
Libra
Sagittarius

Affirmations For The Zodiacs To Balance Their Yin And Yang

Aries: "I **choose** my battles because my energy is **sacred** and not worth spilling over things beyond my control."

Taurus: "I am **flexible** and surrender to **changes** as I know they are for my best and highest self."

Gemini: "Sometimes my **silence** is my **superpower**."

Cancer: "I don't take other people's **opinions** personally as I know it is a **reflection** of them."

Leo: "I make **decisions** from a **soft heart**, not from my ego mind."

Virgo: "I am **perfectly** imperfect."

Libra: "I use my gut to help me make **decisions** and it is simple."

Scorpio: "Everyone is doing the best they can with the **knowledge** they have."

Sagittarius: "I **trust** in divine **timing**."

Capricorn: "My **life** is filled with so much **joy** outside of work, too."

Aquarius: "**Community** is as important for my **soul**, as is alone time."

Pisces: "The **present** is in the **present**."

Heaven

"I am **connected** to the **Heavens**.
I am an **expression** of it after all."

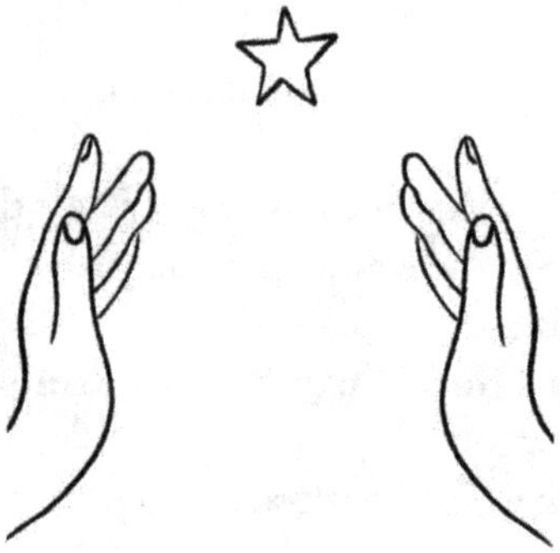

Cielo

"Estoy **conectada** con los **Cielos**.
Soy una **expresión** de ellos."

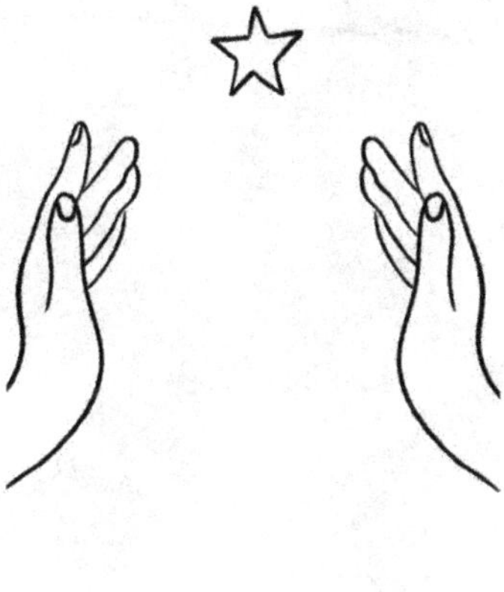

Celestial Guidance

Celestial Guidance

You do not **walk** this **journey** alone.
There is a legion of **ancestors**, **angels** and **divine spirits**
that **walk** with you.
If you ever **feel** fear,
call onto them.
They will make their **presence** known.
Simply say: "Show me you are here with me now."

Ears Ring

Your **ears ring** because they are **whispering words** from Heaven into you
to support you now.

Signs of Celestial Guidance

Finding a **feather** means you're being protected and guided by your angels.

A **song** coming out on the radio that connects with your current life means your angels are hearing what's happening and supporting you.

You drive by a **billboard** that has a special message for you.

You are sent a **message three or more times.**

You see a **picture of an angel** or the word 'angel' somewhere.

The name of a **passed loved** one or something that symbolizes them appears.

Synchronizations.

Finding random **pennies.**

Repeating **numbers.**

Repeating **animals.**

Repeating **words or phrases** that jump out at you.

Receiving a **message related to your situation** from someone that didn't know about it.

Animal Totems

Your angels and guides may send you animal totems to **deliver messages** to you. Sometimes, you might see them in a **dream.** Other times, you may see them **repeated** three or more times in your waking hours. When this happens, it is important to look up the **meaning.** You can also request to see a **specific** animal totem to **communicate** with the Universe on something you'd like to know.

In the next pages, you can find a **glossary** filled with popular totems that the Universe uses to communicate with you. I will also **teach** you how to **communicate** with the Universe using one.

Animal Totems Glossary

A:

Alligator: Reminds you that you are **strong** and can **adapt** to life's current **changes.**

Ant: Shows up to tell you that you have the power to **achieve your goals** as long as you stay persistent.

Antelope: Just like this creature has beautiful **horns** coming out of their **crown chakra** to protect them, you also have a **divine team** that protects you.

B:

Bat: Connect with your **shadow self** and **let go** of fears, anger and limiting behaviors.

Bear: Your spirit needs **time in nature** to recharge.

Beaver: Remember that you have **untapped resources** you can use to **resolve** the matter.

Bee: You have the ability to **build** and achieve **greatness.**

Bobcat: Tap into your **intuition** now. There is information that needs to be shown to you.

Bison: The more you **practice gratitude**, the more **abundance magnifies** for you.

Buffalo: Good things are about to **arrive**. Hang on.

Butterfly: You are in or about to embark into a **transformation** for your **best** and **highest self.**

C:

Cardinal: Associated with **angels** and often signify an **ancestor** is visiting you to tell you they are **present** and **supporting** you.

Caterpillar: It's time to be **patient** and **trust** in divine timing.

Cat: You possess **magic** and can be more **self-reliant.**

Cheetah: Fast-moving changes are happening or about to happen. Remain **focused.**

Chicken: Scratch away at what is being **concealed** from you to discover the **truth.**

Crab: Linked to the **moon,** this **psychic** creature says to connect to your **emotions** and work with the moon energy for **manifesting.**

Crane: Persevere through your current **challenge.** A **happy** outcome is promised as well as **prosperity.**

Coyote: Something is being kept a **secret** and will soon be **revealed.** Trust that your **angels** know this **truth** and will show it to you.

Crocodile: Your **divine team** asks you to **write down** what you need help with so they can bring you that **support.**

D:

Deer: You are **graceful, soft** and **composed.** These are endearing qualities you have and can be **used** for so much more **good.**

Dog: Unconditional love and loyalty surrounds you. It is safe to open your heart as your **purpose** in this **lifetime** is to give and receive **love.**

Dolphin: Have more **playtime.** When you do things you enjoy, you attract more things that are joyful.

Dove: Love is in the air. A happy **union** is coming together. Expect news of a **wedding** soon.

Dragonfly: Reel in **light-heartedness** in your life. A new season of **joy** is unraveling.

Duck: This lovely creature lives both in land and water, showing us to move through life with more **flexibility. Intuition** is another key strength of this animal, reminding you to **trust** yours and **pay attention** to your **surroundings.**

E:

Eagle: Known as the **messenger of the Gods** because it can fly so close to the sun, this **stoic creature** wants you to **trust your intuition,** be a **leader** and resolve the current situation with **grace.**

Elephant: You can **move** any negative force and **obstacle** that stands in your way now of prosperity.

F:

Flamingo: Connect with your **community** more.

Fish: Stop swimming against the current and **allow** life to **flow.**

Fox: You have a **mischievous** and playful character. It's time to **balance** your **inner child** and adult self.

Frog: Ancient wisdom is being downloaded into you This also can be a time of **rebirth** for you.

G:

Goat: Set boundaries with yourself and others.

Giraffe: Tap into your **elegance** and **grace.**

Gorilla: Be more **compassionate with yourself** so that you can be more **understanding with others.**

H:

Horse: Balance your **independence** and duties.

Hippopotamus: Recognize that you are **strong** and believe in your **inner power.**

Hummingbird: Enjoy the sweetness of **life** more.

I:

Iguana: Before making a decision, be sure to **look** at the **situation** from different **angles.**

J:

Jackrabbit: Envision your **future** with **playfulness.** This is a very fertile time to **co-create** with the Universe.

K:

Koala: Symbolizes **peace** and praying more.

Kangaroo: Hop into **action.** Your future is right in front of you, not behind. You also have the presence of **maternal** and **paternal** energies **protecting** you.

L:

Ladybug: Wishes and **dreams** are **coming true** and lady **luck** is on your side now.

Lemur: Stop taking life too seriously and **tap into** your **inner child.**

Leopard: You can **achieve** this dream **alone.** You don't have to worry if you don't have the **support** you need right now. It will come eventually, but you have to start **now.**

Lion: Hone in on your **intelligence** and **tenacity** now. How can you be smarter? How can you **strengthen** your **faith?**

M:

Monkey: Go **socialize,** let loose and **laugh** more. Your health will thank you for it.

Moth: A new cycle of light is commencing for you.

Mouse: Focus on the **present details** so the future can form as you wish.

O:

Octopus: Where do you need to be more **flexible?** Use your **creativity** to **overcome** obstacles.

Ostrich: Your **divine feminine** is **awakening.**

Owl: Guidance to **see** beyond the obvious has arrived. Your **intuition** is strong.

Otter: You need to **rediscover** the things that bring you **joy.**

P:

Panda: Luck and **peace** surround you.

Panther: It is time to **work through** your **fears** and step into your **feminine power.** This gorgeous creature promises you a **rebirth** and can aid you with astral travel and **receiving** messages from the **celestial.**

Parrot: Expect **messages** from Heaven. Pay attention. There are **omens** around you. Additionally, be **careful** who you share **secrets** with because some people like to **gossip.**

Peacock: Start pouring **self-love** into yourself and practicing **affirmations** that elevate your **self-confidence** and **beauty.**

Penguin: Dive down into the calling of your **dreams.** This is also a sign to **work together** with someone or a larger group to **overcome** a problem.

Porcupine: This **playful** spirit asks that you **set boundaries** at this time and re-evaluate what they are. Once they are in place, don't be afraid to **stand up** for yourself if they are crossed.

Puma: Adaptability will give you the **advantage** now. This is a highly **opportunistic** time if you move with **poise.**

Q:

Quail: Making a **swift move** is crucial now. However, it is in your favor to **meditate** and journal on the **pros** and **cons.**

R:

Rat: There is a **truth** you need to see now. Be weary of a **traitor** near you.

Raccoon: You can **survive** this period by using **untapped resources** and people to help you. Another message is that there is someone wearing a **mask** around you and you need to proceed with caution.

Raven: This psychic creature comes to bring you the message that a **metamorphosis** is **coming.**

Rhinoceros: You are **tenacious.** It is time to pick yourself up.

Rooster: You are **courageous** and **good luck** is coming.

S:

Sheep: A part of your **past** needs **TLC** as it is affecting your present self. Also, you are an **individual** and you **don't** need to **conform** to fit in regarding a current situation.

Snake: A **rebirth** is starting or has started. **Shed** your **old** self in order to step into a **better future.**

Seahorse: Small ripples lead to **big waves.** Keep going.

Seal: Spend more **time** with your **family. Place** more **action** into your **intentions.**

Skunk: Set boundaries and protect yourself without **aggressiveness** or violence. **Preserve** your **energy** to create more of what you wish for.

Sloth: Go at your own **pace** with what currently feels **healthy** and **right** to you.

Spider: You are the **weaver** of your own **web** and can spin that web to catch all the **abundance** you wish for. The spider is reminding you that **you create your reality** and you can change it at any time.

Squirrel: Get organized. Save and **prepare** for the **future.**

Stingray: Choose your **battles** wisely.

Swan: You are **graceful** and **elegant.** Love and romance are around the corner.

T:

Tarantula: All your **efforts** are **paying off.** New **doors** are **opening.**

Tiger: Keep your **eye** on the **prize.** There could be a **potential threat,** but you can **handle** it.

Turkey: It is time to **harvest** all the prosperity and **abundance** you have.

Tortoise: Slow and **steady** wins the **race.** Your **consistency** will pay off.

V:

Vulture: Let go of what no longer serves you. This is an omen of new **beginnings.**

W:

Whales: You are **safe** in your **travels** and everything is **working out** in your **favor** now.

Wolf: You are **wise.** Express your **inner truth** and be **cautious** of someone who is being **deceitful.**

Worm: Dig deep. Don't slither away from what's occurring. Ask yourself why is this **happening** to **help** me?

Z:

Zebra: Embrace your **uniqueness** and don't compare yourself to **anyone.** We all have our special **magic** and **moments.**

Monarch Butterfly

A monarch **butterfly greeted** me
outside my parents house one morning.
Hours later,
it **fluttered** onto my balcony
and **watched** me light a **candle**.
Days later,
it **followed** me nearly four thousand miles to Spain.
It was at that **moment**
I knew it had a **message** for me.

Mariposa Monarca

Una **mariposa** monarca me **recibió**
una mañana afuera de la casa de mis padres.
Horas después,
revoloteó hasta mi balcón
y se quedó **mirándome** encender una **vela**.
Días después,
me **siguió** casi cuatro mil millas hasta España.
Fue en ese **momento**
que supe que tenía un **mensaje** para mí.

Message

"If you see an **animal** on your **path** more than **three times**,
it's not a coincidence, there's a **message**
the **Universe** is trying to convey to you."

Mensaje

"Si ves un **animal** en tu **camino** más de **tres veces**,
no es coincidencia, hay un **mensaje**
que el **Universo** intenta transmitirle."

How To Work With An Animal Totem

Select one of your **wishes and goals** that you'd like to know more about.

Second, **choose an animal.** Go with the **first animal** that comes to mind. It should be an animal that you don't often see in your everyday life.

Now, **ask** the Universe to **show** you this **animal** within 24 hours if this intention will manifest. You may see this animal in a photo, hear it in a conversation, read it somewhere or see it on some kind of signage.

If you don't see it within **24 hours**, it means two things. First, that you need to align and work on yourself in order for this intention to manifest. Second, this intention isn't manifesting and something better is coming. *Trust.*

Let's **practice** on the next page.

Setting Intentions with Animal Totems

Set some intentions with animal totems. Make sure to place today's date so you can see how quickly they come to fruition. Check them a month later. It is advised to do no more than two at a time. Otherwise, you may forget.

Example:
My intention is: Travel to Europe
3 details or more about it are: Spain, travel to different cities, fun and happy trip.
The block I am releasing: Not researching and creating an itinerary.
An action I am taking to manifest it is: Create an itinerary and invite someone.
Universe, show me this animal within 24 hours if it will manifest: Owl if I will go to Spain.
Date: 6/5/2024

My intention is:

3 details or more about it are:

The block I am releasing:

An action I am taking to manifest it is:

Universe, show me this animal within 24 hours if it will manifest:

Date:

My intention is:

3 details or more about it are:

The block I am releasing:

An action I am taking to manifest it is:

Universe, show me this animal within 24 hours if it will manifest:

Date:

My intention is:

3 details or more about it are:

The block I am releasing:

An action I am taking to manifest it is:

Universe, show me this animal within 24 hours if it will manifest:

Date:

My intention is:

3 details or more about it are:

The block I am releasing:

An action I am taking to manifest it is:

Universe, show me this animal within 24 hours if it will manifest:

Date:

My intention is:

3 details or more about it are:

The block I am releasing:

An action I am taking to manifest it is:

Universe, show me this animal within 24 hours if it will manifest:

Date:

My intention is:

3 details or more about it are:

The block I am releasing:

An action I am taking to manifest it is:

Universe, show me this animal within 24 hours if it will manifest:

Date:

My intention is:

3 details or more about it are:

The block I am releasing:

An action I am taking to manifest it is:

Universe, show me this animal within 24 hours if it will manifest:

Date:

My intention is:

3 details or more about it are:

The block I am releasing:

An action I am taking to manifest it is:

Universe, show me this animal within 24 hours if it will manifest:

Date:

The Present

Your **presence** is the **present.**
Every day the Universe has a **gift** for you.
It could be a cool **breeze** on your skin.
A moment of **realization through a sunrise.**
The phone ringing with **good news.**
Something so beautiful like a **monarch butterfly** fluttering
a **peacock** sauntering through your backyard or
the chirps of a **red cardinal** perched on a tree saying hello.
The healing **embrace** of a loved one that melts away
your rigid mind like chocolate chip cookies in an oven
and leaves you with the **sweetest feeling** inside knowing
that **everything** is going to be **alright**. It always has.
It always will. The things we worry about never happen.
That's why your presence is the present.
Not the past nor the future which is actually being created in the present.
If you are willing to **let go** of the distractions
You will be **rewarded** every day.

El Presente

Tu **presencia** es el **presente.**
Cada día el Universo tiene un **regalo** para ti.
Podría ser una **brisa** fresca en tu piel.
Un momento de **realización a través de un amanecer**.
El teléfono suena con **buenas noticias.**
Algo tan hermoso como una **mariposa monarca** revoloteando
un **pavo real** paseando por su patio trasero o
los chirridos de un **cardenal rojo** posado en un árbol saludando.
El **abrazo** sanador de un ser querido que se derrite
tu mente rígida como galletas con chispas de chocolate en un horno.
y te deja con **la sensación más dulce** en tu interior al saber
que **todo** va a estar **bien**. Siempre lo ha sido.
Siempre lo será. Las cosas que nos preocupan nunca suceden.
Por eso tu presencia es el presente.
Ni el pasado ni el futuro que en realidad se está creando en el
presente.
Si estás dispuesto a **dejar de lado** las distracciones
Serás **recompensado** todos los días.

Sign

"I am ready to **receive** my **signs** that show me my **future**."

Señal

"Estoy listo para **recibir** mis **señales** que me muestran mi **futuro.**"

Plants, Flowers, And Other Totems

Your angels and guides will also send you **other totems** such as **plants, flowers and objects** to get your attention. Sometimes, you might see it in a **dream**. Other times, you may see it **repeated three** or more times in your **waking hours**. When this happens, it is important to look up the meaning. To communicate with the Universe, you can also request to see a **specific plant, flower or an object**, such as a rainbow, an ice cream cone or a blue piece of cake. This can help you confirm as to whether something is going to manifest or not.

The format is the same as with the animal totems. So you'll get the hang of it easily in the next pages. Again, if you don't see the sign within 24 hours, it might not come to fruition because something better is on the horizon for you or you simply are not aligned for it yet.

Example:
My intention is: To launch a new lucrative business.
3 details or more about it are: Work remotely, fun, and earns me the perfect amount that makes my heart happy.
The block I am releasing: Letting go of procrastination
An action I am taking to manifest it is: Brainstorm and asking the Universe to show me what is for my best and highest self.
Universe, show me this plant, flower or object: Monchhichi doll
Date: 6/9/24

My intention is:

3 details or more about it are:

The block I am releasing:

An action I am taking to manifest it is:

Universe, show me this plant, flower or object within 24 hours if it will manifest:

Date:

My intention is:

3 details or more about it are:

The block I am releasing:

An action I am taking to manifest it is:

Universe, show me this plant, flower or object within 24 hours if it will manifest:

Date:

My intention is:

3 details or more about it are:

The block I am releasing:

An action I am taking to manifest it is:

Universe, show me this plant, flower or object within 24 hours if it will manifest:

Date:

My intention is:

3 details or more about it are:

The block I am releasing:

An action I am taking to manifest it is:

Universe, show me this plant, flower or object within 24 hours if it will manifest:

Date:

My intention is:

3 details or more about it are:

The block I am releasing:

An action I am taking to manifest it is:

Universe, show me this plant, flower or object within 24 hours if it will manifest:

Date:

My intention is:

3 details or more about it are:

The block I am releasing:

An action I am taking to manifest it is:

Universe, show me this plant, flower or object within 24 hours if it will manifest:

Date:

My intention is:

3 details or more about it are:

The block I am releasing:

An action I am taking to manifest it is:

Universe, show me this plant, flower or object within 24 hours if it will manifest:

Date:

My intention is:

3 details or more about it are:

The block I am releasing:

An action I am taking to manifest it is:

Universe, show me this plant, flower or object within 24 hours if it will manifest:

Date:

My intention is:

3 details or more about it are:

The block I am releasing:

An action I am taking to manifest it is:

Universe, show me this plant, flower or object within 24 hours if it will manifest:

Date:

Chocolate Croissant

"I asked the Universe to show me a **chocolate croissant** if I would go to the **city of love** again and it did. Now, I am sitting in a cafe, watching Parisians stroll by and am about to meet the **love of my life**."

Croissant De Chocolate

"Le pedí al Universo que me mostrara un **croissant de chocolate** si volvería a ir a la **ciudad del amor** y así fue. Ahora estoy sentada en un café viendo pasar a los Parisinos y estoy a punto de conocer al **amor de mi vida.**"

Totem Review

Remember the Universe will send you totems
and you can also ask for specific ones.

What Is An Angel Number?

Angel numbers are **messages** from your **angels**. Each number has a special **meaning**. You can see angel numbers everywhere. Some popular places to spot them are on a **clock, an address, a receipt or a wall**. When one appears to you, it is your angels letting you know they are right **beside** you and that they want you to **look up** the meaning of the number they are showing you.

¿Qué Es Un Número Angelical?

Los números de ángeles son **mensajes** de tus **ángeles**. Cada número tiene un **significado** especial. Puedes ver números de ángeles en todas partes. Algunos lugares populares para verlos son en un **reloj, una dirección, un recibo o una pared**. Cuando se te aparece uno, son tus ángeles haciéndote saber que están justo **a tu lado** y que quieren que **busques** el significado del número que te muestran.

Angel Numbers And Their Meanings

111: New beginnings + tuning in with your spiritual side.

222: Surrender to the flow + trust the process. New opportunities.

333: Encouragement. Time to make essential changes.

444: Release doubts + keep moving forward in faith.

555: Major life changes are manifesting.

666: Re-examine your life + get into a better alignment.

777: Self-awareness has increased. A break-through will occur soon.

888: Abundance is materializing

999: Forgiveness. Release control + accept the reality of a certain situation. End of a chapter.

1010: Everything is working out for you. Moving towards higher purpose.

1111: Make wishes. We all are one.
Keep your mind optimistic as what we think, we become.

1212: Luck in love. Obstacles are being removed.

1313: Believe in yourself, you are amazing and talented.

1414: Reexamine your foundations and make necessary changes.

1515: Stay motivated because things are going to start to look up.

1616: A profound change is around the corner.

1717: Take responsibility for your choices.
You have more influence over your life patterns.

1818: Changes are happening that are taking you to your life purpose.

1919: If you have been praying for big dreams, this is your sign that one or more are happening. This is going to change your life.

2020: Positive momentum is on the horizon. This can mean partnerships.

Seasons

Gift

"The Universe **communicates** with me daily
and I am present to **receive** the **gifts** it has for me today."

Regalo

"El Universo se **comunica** conmigo a diario y estoy presente para **recibir** los **regalos** que hoy tiene para mí."

Chapter

"Each **season** marks a new **chapter** in your life.
Beautiful months to **fill** up with the most extraordinary **dreams**
and simple **pleasures** that make life **sweet**. I hope that you **write**
the most beautiful **story** filled with a lot of **joy**."

Capítulo

"Cada **temporada** marca un nuevo **capítulo** en tu vida.
Hermosos meses para **llenarte** de los **sueños** más extraordinarios
y de los **placeres** sencillos que **endulzan** la vida. Espero que **escribas**
la **historia** más hermosa y llena de mucha **alegría.**"

Spring Equinox To-Knows

Night and day are **equal** in length.

Write a **gratitude** list for the winter season and highlight your **peaks** and **lessons.**

This is a time of **rebirth.** Write what you're birthing into existence now.

It is in **Yang** energy, which is **action** energy.

Make a **4-column list** with March, April, May and June heading each column. Below each month write the **wishes** you want to manifest.

Make a **release** list of what you are leaving behind in winter.

Get **fresh flowers** and plants to **celebrate** this new time.

Spend time outdoors recharging your **aura**.

Spring clean to raise the energy in your space.

Light a candle and use the **Spring Equinox Prayer** from *My Little Prayer Book: 75 Prayers, Poems & Mantras for Illumination*.

Wear **white** to represent a **new beginning.**

Summer Solstice To-Knows

Decorate your space with **seasonal flowers**, like sunflowers.

Self-reflect on what you gained and learned during the **Spring** season.

It is in **Yang** energy, which is **action** energy. Think about what action you will take now to reach goals.

Make a **4-column list** with June, July, August and September heading each column. Below each month write the **wishes** you want to manifest.

Make an **"I let go" list** of what you want to release and **burn it**.

Clean and organize home to clear stagnant energy. Use **citrus essential oils**.

Use the **sun symbol**, recharge in the sun and make a **sunwheel**.

Work with **citrine**, carnelian, amber and crystals connected to the sun.

Prepare a delicious meal, maybe a **picnic** using seasonal fruits and veggies.

Light a candle and use the **Summer Solstice Prayer** from *My Little Prayer Book: 75 Prayers, Poems & Mantras for Illumination*.

Wear yellow, orange, red or gold to represent the season of the sun.

Fall Equinox To-Knows

It is connected with **Yin energy**.

It is about **softness**, stillness and reflection.

It is a good time to welcome **restorative** energy.

Chakras ignited are heart, sacral, third eye and crown.

Self-reflect on the summer season, what **lessons** it taught you and how you have **grown**.

Make a **5-column list** with September, October, November and December heading each column. Below each month write the **wishes** you want to manifest for each month.

Get an **apple** and place a coin next to it to call in **prosperity**.

Visit a pumpkin patch, farmer's market or spend time **outdoors** recharging with the season.

Decorate your space with **elements of this season**, like pumpkins, fall leaves and seasonal fruits, which bring abundance and luck.

Enjoy a nice spiced tea or coffee and **drink with intention**. Think of what you're grateful for.

Boil cinnamon to reel in abundance. Read intentions and toss in. Let the energy soak your intentions with good energy. Make sure to keep a copy.

Cut hair to let go of old energy.

Winter Solstice To-Knows

It is when the **shortest day** and **longest night** occur.

Cultures around the globe celebrate this time of year as a **return to the light** because we begin to inch our way back into the light.

It is referred to by many as **Yule.**

It is filled with **Yin magic**, which helps co-create your life with **gentleness.**

Light a candle to celebrate the return to the light.
Say, "*I welcome more light into my life and my intentions.*"

Make a **table wreath** to symbolize the natural cycle of life. Then insert four candles inside to represent the **four directions of the elements** and how they will bring blessings and alignment to your life now.

Decorate a tree with ornaments like stars, the sun and the moon to represent the cosmic guiding force in our lives. Also, place photos of loved ones to honor them.

Write a Fall Release Letter. List everything you wish to let go of so that you can start this new season with good intentions.

Spend time outdoors. Grab a ball of snow, make a wish and toss it into the air. Snow is magic just like water.

Make a **4-column list** with December, January, February and March heading each column. Below each month write the **wishes** you want to manifest.

Bring in seasonal elements such as Holly, which is known to ward off negative energy and remove blocks. Use Mistletoe to invite in love. Poinsettias are perfect to plant intentions with.

Inner Child Healing

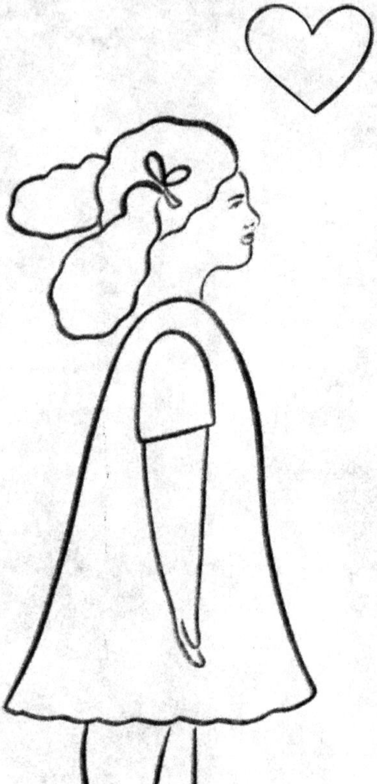

Heal Your Inner Child

Your **inner child** exists in you during your entire **lifetime**. There are events from your **childhood** that left **scars.** These can trickle into your adult life and prevent you from obtaining certain **goals** or living with inner **peace.** Present you has the ability to return to the past and **heal** that child. This, in turn, will **alter** your **timeline** and help you step into the **future version** you **dream** of. There are inner child **meditations**, holistic therapy and other modalities, like journaling and affirmations, that can help you **achieve** this.

Cocoon

"**Build** yourself a **cocoon** to heal in,
and then **emerge** out of it as a **butterfly**."

Capullo

"**Construyete** un **capullo** para curarte
y luego **emerge** de él como una **mariposa.**"

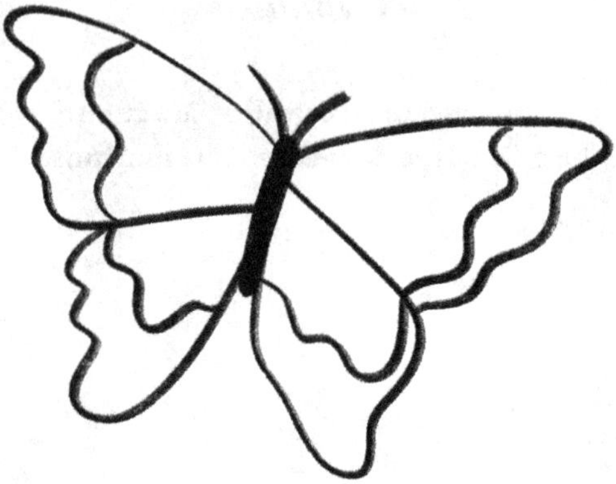

Your Own Pace

Healing is not linear. There is **no** time **limit** on how long it can take to get over a person or experience. Go at the **pace** your soul needs. Do the **soft** things your **spirit** calls for. You deserve to **nurture** yourself. We often want to rush out of the **experience** and discomfort, but that can stunt our **growth** and not allow us to fully grasp the **lesson** of the experience. Remember to **build** yourself a beautiful **cocoon** so, when you're done **healing**, you can emerge out as a **butterfly**.

Inner Child Letter Meditation

The **inner child letter meditation** is a very healing meditation that **bridges** the gap between your **past, present and future**. It is a simple yet very profound meditation. You will be able to **receive messages** from **little you** on what she needs from adult you now. This, in turn, will **nourish** your mind, body and spirit and help you co-create a healthy, confident and peaceful future you. We are going to create the letter on the next few pages. This way, we can keep it somewhere safe and you can return to read it and witness your progress.

Instructions:

Light a candle. Get a **photo** of little **you.**

Tape/paste the photo in the box on the following page.

Now, write a **list of 20 things** adult you is promising little you.

This **list** can **encompass** anything little you **needs.**
Some examples are speaking kindly to myself, advocating for little me, completing certain goals/projects, pursuing a hobby or having an experience little you always wanted to have.
Write what comes to heart and mind.

(Place your photo above)

I love and adore little me so much.
I am creating these pages for her to make her
dreams and needs come to fruition through adult me.

20 Things I Promise Little Me:

How did you like the **inner child letter meditation**?

What did you **learn** while **creating** it?

Self-Love Compliment List For Little You

Little you may have heard some things that hurt her and that challenged her **self-worth**. As children, we don't always have the tools to process and heal. Today, we are going to take our **power** back for our past selves and show them how valuable, incredible and **magnificent** they are. We are going to do this by making a list of 25 **beautiful** things we can praise little us for.

Make a list of **25 beautiful compliments** little you needs to hear now.

Slow Dancing

I am slow **dancing**
with my shadow **self**,
allowing her to **move** out
of her **darkness**,
giving her **permission** with
each step to **turn**
and turn where the **stars**
sparkle,
where shame and **grief**
from **past** choices
no longer have to be **heavy**
secrets
that weigh her **down**
but **free** her forward
to **rise** towards her **dreams.**

Intuitive Dancing Meditation For Joy

Dancing is an easy way to **open up** your **'joy' chakra** and get you instantaneous results. The joy chakra is known as the **sacral chakra** and it resides in your **pelvic area**. It is connected to your **creativity** and **pleasure**. Are you looking for an innovative way to solve a problem or make something? Need to laugh, let go and remember what to be happy about? Want to reignite and find your passion again? This very intuitive meditation asks you to put on your favorite music, **listen** to it and **move** as you feel called to. Your body will **show you** what it needs.

Instructions:

Choose a **space** where you have **privacy**.

Light a **candle** or some **sacred smoke**.

Press **play** on your favorite **music**.

Start off by **warming up** your body with some **stretching**.

Start **dancing** as you **feel** called to.

Your **body** will **tell** you **intuitively** what it needs and where there is stuck energy it is desiring to release.

Do this for about **20 minutes**.

Drink **water**.

Be prepared to **receive messages** after.

Ignited

"'**I believe in you.**' She whispered these **words** to herself and it **ignited** her soul on fire again."

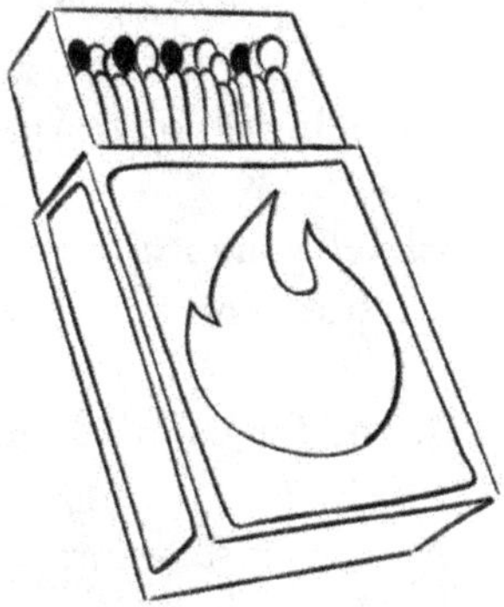

Encendido

"'**Creo en ti.**' Ella se susurró estas **palabras** para sí misma y eso **encendió** su alma de nuevo."

Girl On Fire

Whisper to the little **girl**
who is **standing** in the **hallways**
of your **heart**, waiting for
someone to **believe** in her.
I believe in her.

Whisper to the little **girl**.
The one who was told to **sit** down
and stay as **silent** as a secret
because her **voice** didn't matter.
I'm speaking up for her.

Whisper to the little **girl**
whose tiny **light** extinguished
because **she** was told
she wasn't **good** enough.
We are setting this world on fire now
and making our dreams happen.

Inner Fires

Inner fires are dangerous because nobody knows your burning alive with your own **thoughts**. And the only way to **extinguish** them is to stand in the shower letting the droplets tap tap tap all over your skin and talk to you. *"Hello. Open up! You can't let this consume you."* And when you finally give in, you break into convulsions, **letting** out long, guttural cries that make you sound more animal than **woman**. Perhaps, this is the wolf in you **howling**. Your warm salty tears blend with the **water**, and all of a sudden, you realize, for an instant, you have **become** one with this element. You, too, are an **ocean**, after all. Slowly now, gently, the **waves** that came crashing out of you have subsided. You have once again healed yourself and begun to **flow**.

Beginning

"We **women** are just like the **New Moon**,
glowing and **growing** through cycles,
learning to **love** ourselves
with every new **beginning**."

Comienzo

"Nosotras **mujeres** somos como la **luna nueva**,
brillando y **creciendo** a través de ciclos,
aprendiendo a **amarnos** a nosotras mismas
con cada nuevo **comienzo.**"

New Moons

How New Moons Can Help You

New Moons are my favorite lunar occurrence. Once a month, there is a New Moon. They represent a **new cycle in your life**. I find that intentions rapidly manifest in this lunar period. Most people hype up the Full Moon because they can see it. However, just because you can't see something doesn't mean it doesn't exist or it isn't just as powerful. In fact, **New Moons** are the more **favorable** and **potent** of the two when it comes to starting a new cycle and **planting new seeds**.

New Moon Symptoms

Awareness

Faster manifestations

Heightened intuition

Wanting to reset

Desire to reach new levels

Relaxation

Grounding

Sense of direction

New Moon Checklist

Use this checklist 3 days before or up until 3 days after
to complete the rituals that call to you.

Clean and organize your space to create harmony and open your space to receive the abundance you desire.

Use sacred smoke or essential oils to refresh. Walk around your space and say, *"I release energy that doesn't serve me and I replace it with flow."*

Light a candle and set intentions. New Moons are a new cycle.
Ask yourself what would you like to start new.
What new level are you ready to step into?

New Moon Intention:
"Thank you Universe for this new abundance in my life. I am so grateful for it."

Journal. Think about what's changed from last New Moon to now.
Make a list of what's different.

Work with the **element** the **moon** is in.

Pray. Use the *My Little Prayer Book: 75 Prayers, Poems and Mantras for Illumination* New Moon Prayer.

Meditate.

Make **New Moon water** by placing a jar/bowl outside or by a windowsill filled with water. Then, the following day, sprinkle it around your space and on yourself to refresh the energy.

Work on your Vision Book. Add and tweak your vision for the year.

Get guidance on a question and **pull some cards.**

Set **crystals to charge** outside or by a windowsill.

New Moon Meditation

Light a candle for **guidance.**
Say: "Universe, I welcome my fresh new cycle."

Burn incense or **palo santo** to **purify** your space.
Say: "My space is ready to receive blessings."

Write some intentions you'd like to experience in this cycle.
Say: "I am ready to receive these intentions and be guided to them."

Journal about the last 30 days. What were your peaks and pits?
Say: "I am grateful for my last 30 day journey.
I know the best is yet to come."

Place one hand on the heart and the other on your belly.
Take 3 inhales and exhales.
Say: "I support this new beginning."

Keep one hand on your heart and the other on your belly.
Say: "I am braver today."

Stay with one hand on your heart and the other on your belly.
Say: "I am following my heart now."

Continue in the same position.
Say: "I love how strong my faith is."

Read your intentions.
Say: "Thank you Universe for helping me co-create these intentions."

Make **New Moon water** and sprinkle it around your space.

Different New Moons

Every month, a New Moon rises in a different element. It is important to know what element the moon is in so you can work with that energy.

Air Moon

Connects you with: Future innovation.

Do: Open windows to bring freshness in and future messages. Spend time outdoors feeling the wind on your face, write yourself a letter from your future self, practice automatic writing.

Earth Moon

Connects you with: Grounding.

Do: Get a pedicure, reflexology, spend time walking barefoot, bring fresh flowers and plants into your space, go forest bathing, spend time in nature.

Fire Moon

Connects you with: Renewal energy, rebirth.

Do: Burn sacred smoke, write a burn letter, burn a bay leaf, work with sunflowers that connect with the sun, make a list of actions to back up your intentions.

Water Moon

Connects you with: Psychic messages, dream world, emotions.

Do: Shower meditation, healing baths, swim, ocean wading, release a bay leaf in the ocean.

Palo Santo Yourself Meditation

Palo Santo, which translates to "**holy wood**," is an incredible tool to keep the positive energy locked into your space. When things are going well, you can **amplify** it and raise your **aura** by lighting Palo Santo. This beautiful meditation is ideal to use for the **New Moon**.

Light your **Palo Santo**.

Close your **eyes** or cast them down.

Take a deep **breath in** and hold it till the count of five and **exhale**.

Open your **eyes**. Now, begin to **trace** your **silhouette**, chakra by chakra.

Start at the top of our head. Move **clockwise** and then **counterclockwise**.

Say: "*I am guided to fresh new ideas and opportunities.*"

Move the **wand** to your **third eye**. Move clockwise and then counterclockwise.

Say: "*I can see my new cycle is full of bigger blessings than I can imagine.*"

Place the **wand** at your **throat**. Move clockwise and then counterclockwise.

Say: "*It is easy to manifest right now.*"

Now, carry the **wand** to your **heart**. Move clockwise and then counterclockwise.

Say: "*I love my life and my life loves me back.*"

Gently, place the **wand** by your **belly**. Move clockwise and then counterclockwise.

Say: "*I take back my power now and open new doors.*"

Ignite your joy by pointing the **Palo Santo** towards your **pelvic area** and moving it clockwise and then counterclockwise.

Say: "*My happiness doubles daily.*"

Ground by taking the **Palo Santo** stick to your **legs** and bottom of your **feet**. Move it up and down clockwise and counterclockwise.

Say: "*My new path leads me exactly where I wish to go.*"

Dreams

"**Objects** are **closer** than they appear.
Your **dreams** are **materializing**."

Sueños

"Los **objetos** están más **cerca** de lo que parecen.
Tus **sueños** se están **materializando.**"

"The **New Moon** is your new **beginning.**"

"La **luna nueva** es tu nuevo **comienzo.**"

Wise Women, Mujeres Sabia

This chapter is about realizing the wise woman within.
So many stories of wise women in your lineage run through your veins.
Here, you will open the door to connect with more of them.

Wise Woman

I am a **wise woman.**
In my blood, I carry the **ancient wisdom** from
all the women in my **lineage.**
This wisdom is **accessible** to me at all times.
I can **find** it when I ask for it.
It comes to me in
dreams,
messages from **loved ones,**
journaling,
meditation,
prayer,
nature,
books,
music,
and when I open my **heart like a door**
and **listen** to what it **needs.**

Mujer Sabia

Soy una **mujer sabia.**
En mi sangre, llevo la **sabiduría ancestral** de
todas las mujeres de mi **linaje.**
Esta sabiduría es **accesible** para mí en todo momento.
Puedo **encontrarlo** cuando lo pida.
Me viene en
sueños,
mensajes de **seres queridos,**
llevar un diario,
meditación,
oración,
naturaleza,
libros,
música,
y cuando abro mi **corazón como una puerta**
y **escucho** lo que **necesita.**

Clock

"**Divine timing** is the only clock
I have learned that **counts.**"

Reloj

"El **tiempo divino** es el único reloj
que he aprendido que **cuenta.**"

Divine Timing

You will **find me** through
a trail of **prayers** lit with candles
and handwritten **notes** in churches and temples.
I have not lost **faith** in myself
even though sometimes
I have wanted to.
Divine timing is the only **clock**
I have learned that **counts.**
I **trust** that when it is meant to be
It will be for **me.**

Tiempo Divino

Me **encontrarás** a través de
un camino de **oraciones** iluminado con velas
y **notas** escritas a mano en iglesias y templos.
No he perdido la **fe** en mi misma
aunque a veces
he querido.
El tiempo **divino** es el único **reloj**
que he aprendido **cuenta.**
Confío en que cuando esté destinado a ser
será para **mí.**

The Divine Feminine

"The wise woman knows that when she is in
her **soft energy** this is when she is her **strongest**.
She doesn't have to force anything
because **life flows** for her when she allows it to."

"La mujer sabia sabe que cuando está en
su **energía suave** es cuando es más **fuerte**.
No tiene que forzar nada porque la **vida fluye**
para ella cuando ella lo permite."

I Am, Yo Soy

I am in my **soft feminine era**.
I am **creator** of *mi vida*.
I am ***agua*** flowing gently.
I am a soft breeze kissing your cheeks.
I am, *yo soy*.

She Is An Alchemist

She is an **alchemist.**
Her **tears** transmuted into her greatest **strength.**
The **put-downs** morphed into her **confidence.**
Years of **silence** transformed into **assertiveness.**
She had **learned** only she could **validate** herself.
And in doing so, she has been **reborn** a **fierce tigress,**
roaring with **self-love.**
Mysterious, unapologetically beautiful like a **scarlet rose**
and **brave** to go after what drummed in her **heart.**
Oh, to finally **listen** to her **heart.**
That's where her **truth** was and that is where **yours** is, too.

Ella Es Una Alquimista

Ella es una **alquimista.**
Sus **lágrimas** se transmutaron en su mayor **fortaleza.**
Las **críticas** se transformaron en su **confianza.**
Años de **silencio** se transformaron en **asertividad.**
Había **aprendido** que solo ella podía **validarse** a sí misma.
Y al hacerlo, habia **renacida** coma una **feroz tigresa**
rugiendo de **amor propio.**
Misteriosa, hermosa sin complejos como una rosa escarlata
y **valiente** para ir tras lo que latía en su **corazón.**
Oh, **escuchar** finalmente a su **corazón.**
Ahí es donde estaba su **verdad** y ahí es donde está la **tuya** también.

Your Light Divine Feminine: What To Know

One half of your **divine feminine.**

Acknowledges and healthily **processes emotions.**

Comfortable embracing life.

Nurturing energy.

Forgiving and **compassionate** towards yourself and others.

Graceful even in **challenging moments.**

Soft and **powerful.**

Reflective and **creative.**

Wise and **heart-centered.**

Peacemaker.

Embraces **intuition.**

Your Dark Divine Feminine: What To Know

One half of your **divine feminine**.

Authentic in all you do.

Aligned action based on what's best for your highest self.

Able to **alchemize negative situations** into positive ones.

Comfortable being **assertive.**

Confident.

Embraces her **sexuality**.

Fearless.

Mysterious.

Protective of loved ones.

Treats others as **equal.**

Two Sides

"There are **two sides** to a **healed woman**.
This is her light like a **sunrise** bringing us morning
and her darkness like a **sunset** taking us to evening."

Dos Lados

"Hay **dos lados** de una **mujer sanada.**
Esta es su luz como un **amanecer** que nos trae la mañana
y su oscuridad como un **atardecer** que nos lleva a la noche."

Whole, Not Broken

An **unhealed** woman carries **wounds**
she must heal in order to live freely.
These traumas are **inherited** from **generations** past.
Some are **genetically** passed down
and some are the **collective** energy.
Women's oppression, marginalization
and the silencing of women throughout time
created these **bruises** in you.
It is up to you now to do the **work** of
self-loving, validating and liberating yourself.
You are meant to be whole, not broken.

Completa, No Rota

Una mujer **sin curar** carga con **heridas**
que debe curar para poder vivir libremente.
Estos traumas se **heredan** de **generaciones** pasadas.
Algunos se transmiten **genéticamente**
y otros son energía **colectiva.**
La opresión, la marginación y el silenciamiento
de las mujeres a lo largo del tiempo
crearon estos **morados** en ti.
Ahora depende de ti hacer el **trabajo** de
amarte a ti misma, validarte y liberarte.
Estás destinada a estar completa, no rota.

The Wounded Feminine

Comparing themselves to others.

Not feeling good enough or **worthy**.

Damsel in distress.

Drama (every couple of weeks, something will come up).

Disconnection from our **authentic self.**

Difficulty **expressing needs**.

Entitlement.

Envy.

Emotional numbness.

Fear of **vulnerability**.

Feeling like a **child**/powerless.

Guilt.

Hopelessness.

Imposter syndrome.

Silent treatment.

Self-doubt.

Self-blame.

Tantrums.

Unhealthy relationship **patterns.**

Victimhood.

Waiting for someone to come and **save** her.

How To Start Healing Your Wounded Feminine

Identify Your Wounds:
Notice your triggers, limiting behaviors and patterns.
Action:
Keeping a diary of your emotions will help you to heal.

Set Boundaries:
Set boundaries and begin to put yourself and your needs first.
Action:
Make a 2-column list of what is currently draining you and then reflect on what you need.

Self-Care:
Set time to pause, rest and do activities that rejuvenate your soul.
Action:
Read a prayer book, meditate, journal and exercise.
Splurge on a massage, acupuncture or a reiki session.

Self-Validation:
Work on activities that teach you self-validation.
Action:
Write yourself a loving letter explaining why you are proud of yourself.
Make a self-compliment jar and write one compliment a day to yourself.
Work with an affirmation list or deck.

Connect with Feminine Activities:
Journal about when you feel your most soft feminine.
Action:
Buy yourself flowers, journal, paint, draw, take a pottery or cooking class, garden, read, sign up for a photography course, learn how to make jewelry, practice yoga or do a dance class.

Journal Regularly:
This will help you connect with you.
Action:
Write about anything that comes to mind.
Let yourself be free when you write.

Spend Time in Nature:
Nature is very healing.
It can help to activate your intuition and bring you guidance.
Action:
Go to the beach, sit at a park with a book or go for a walk.

Inner Child Healing:
Connect with little you and what she needs to hear and heal in order to become divine you.
Action:
Make a list of things little you needed.
Then, start to check off as you give these things to her.
Try an inner child meditation.

Use Affirmations:
Practice repeating affirmations that give you strength, peace and good energy.
Action:
Invest in a deck or write some of your own affirmations.
Examples are "I am good enough,"
"I am worthy of great things"
and "I believe in myself."

Affirmations For Divine Feminine Power

I am a **divine** feminine power.

I am **intuitive**.

I am **confident**.

I am good **enough**.

I am **beautiful** inside and out.

I am **assertive**.

I **believe** in myself.

I am **worthy** of greatness.

I am **authentic** and it is safe to be me.

I am a **wise** woman.

I am **soft** and **strong**.

I am **creative** and **talented**.

I **validate** myself.

I allow myself to **give** and **receive** pleasure.

I love my **goddess** body, face and spirit.

I **honor** all the stages of me.

Divine Karmic Exchange

When it comes to relationships, it is important to measure the **karmic exchange** between you and the people in your life.

For **divine karma**, the exchange should be an **equal amount** of **giving** and **receiving.**

Desert Rose

A **desert rose** is simply a **woman**
who knows how to **bloom** in
in the harshest **conditions.**

Rosa Del Desierto

Una **rosa del desierto** es simplemente una **mujer**
quién sabe **florecer**
en las **condiciones** más duras.

Prayer

"In the name of the **mother**,
the **daughter** and the **holy spirit**."

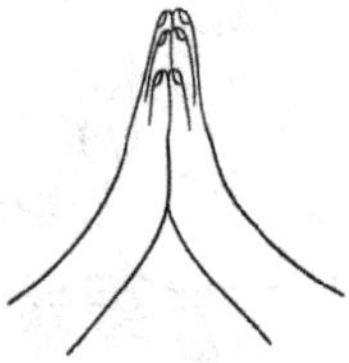

Oración

"En el nombre de la **madre**,
de la **hija** y del **espíritu santo.**"

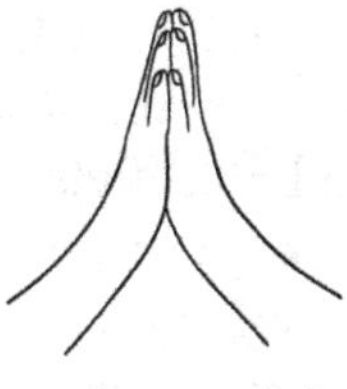

Heavenly Stretch Mark Blessed

Some of us **women**
have been
heavenly **stretch mark** blessed.
We've been **painted** by the **angels**
and anointed
with **ethereal** lines
that **glisten** and **sparkle**
in hues of silver and white
across our **bodies**
like **constellations**.

Heavenly stretch mark blessed.
Oh yes, we have these
sacred gifts emblazoned on us
for a lifetime.
Divine tattoos dancing along our skin,
reminding us to **celebrate** and honor
how much our bodies **do** for us.
How much our bodies **heal** for us.
How much our bodies **fight** for us just to
grow, expand, glitter
and exist.
Heavenly stretch marked blessed.

What **features** from your **body** are your **favorite**?

Did you know that when you **speak loving kind words** to your body, those words are **vibrating** into your **cells** and helping you stay **healthy** within?

How do **you feel** about **stretch marks**?

How do **you feel** about **wrinkles, cellulite** and other **natural occurrences** on the human body?

Are you **comfortable with aging** or is it something you need to work on? If so, what exactly would you like to work on **accepting**?

Storm

"She is **thunder**. She is **lightning**.
She is not afraid to be a **storm**."

Tormenta

"Ella es un **trueno**. Ella es un **relampago**.
Ella no tiene miedo de ser una **tormenta.**"

Thunder Thighs

You called me **thunder thighs**
like it was a bad thing to
to **walk** into rooms loudly with my
God-given body.

Thunder thighs.
Oh me, oh my.
Why should I apologize for my **curves**
that move from side to side like a
delicious disco beat?

Thunder thighs.
Oh me, oh my.
Honey, I wasn't made
to **squeeze** into a certain **size**
or be a **goal weight**
or deprive myself from **enjoying life**.
I did that far too long when
you convinced me to
hate these **thighs**.

Thunder thighs.
Oh me, oh my.
I am no longer a hushed **rainstorm**.
I'm a **make-the-ground-shake**,
with **confidence**
thunderstorm,
here to leave you **thunderstruck**.

Oh me, oh my.

Lines

The **lines** all over your body
are **maps** to where you have been.
True **beauty marks.**
Don't erase them. They are the **stories** that
took you through **places** to get to
who you are today. **Retrace** them
whenever you doubt **yourself**
so you can **remember** how far you've come.

Lineas

Las **líneas** por todo tu cuerpo
Son **mapas** de donde has estado.
Verdaderas **marcas de belleza**.
No los borres. Son las **historias** que
te llevó a través de **lugares** para llegar
quién eres hoy. **Volver** sobre ellos
cada vez que dudas de **ti misma**
para que puedas **recordar** hasta dónde has llegado.

"**Wise** women always **follow**
their **heart** chakra—their inner **compass.**"

"Las mujeres **sabias** siempre **siguen**
su chakra del **corazón**—su **brújula** interior."

The Chakras

What Are Chakras?

Chakras are spinning **energetic wheels** inside different points of your body. When one is blocked, it can prevent you from achieving your goals. We have **seven main chakras** in the body.

Refer to the chart on the next page to learn more about your chakras.

7 Main Chakras Chart

Crown
Location: Top of your head | **Color:** Purple or white.
Purpose: Connects you with the Universe to bring you the guidance + direction you need.
Crystals: Amethyst + Crystal Quartz.
Flowers: Lavender, Petunia, Pansy + Sweet Peas.

Third Eye
Location: In between your eyebrows | **Color:** Indigo
Purpose: Opens your eyes literally. Gives you clarity + helps you tap into your intuition.
Crystals: Lapis Lazuli.
Flowers: Blue Orchid, Blue Hibiscus, Wild Indigo, Salvia + Hydrangea.

Throat
Location: Throat | **Color:** Baby Blue
Purpose: Aligns your inner + external voice so that you can manifest. (Remember, both need to be aligned in order to reel in your intentions.)
Crystals: Blue Sodalite.
Flowers: Anemone, Forget-Me-Nots + Morning Glory.

Heart
Location: Heart | **Color:** Pink for self-love. Green for other kinds of love.
Purpose: Opens your heart to give + receive love freely without expectations.
Crystals: Green Aventurine + Malachite.
Flowers: Calla Lily, Carnation, Chrysanthemum + Dahlia.

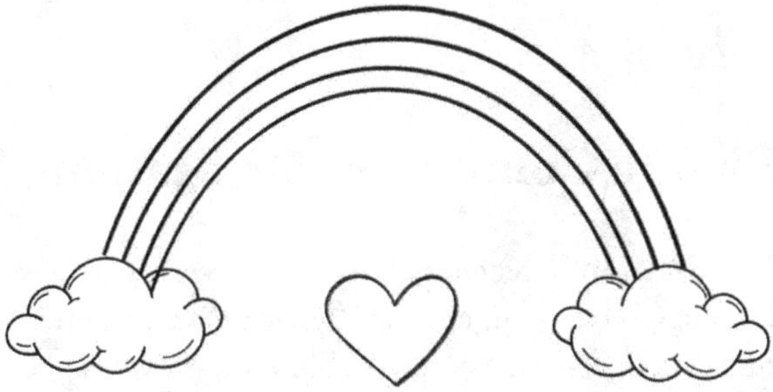

Solar Plexus
Location: Stomach | **Color:** Yellow
Purpose: Powers up your strength, inner confidence + reminds you of your limitless opportunities.
Crystals: Citrine.
Flowers: Begonia, Black-Eyed Susan, Daisy, Sunflower + Wishbone Flower.

Sacral
Location: Pelvis | **Color:** Orange
Purpose: Invigorates your joy, creativity + pleasure.
Crystals: Carnelian, Fire Agate, Goldstone, Orange Aventurine + Red Jasper.
Flowers: Ballerina Tulip, Chinese Lantern, Gerber Daisy + Marigold.

Root
Location: Legs + feet | **Color:** Red
Purpose: Sparks grounding, reminds you that you are safe, secure + your basics needs are being met.
Crystals: Garnet, Red Jasper, + Onyx.
Flowers: Bee Balm, Bleeding Heart, Dahlia, Geranium, Poppy + Rose.

Chakra Connection Meditation

This **beautiful meditation** I created will help you easily **get messages** from each of your chakras. To begin, light a candle, or *velita*. Put on a meditation song to help you **relax** and sit in a comfortable spot. Now, let's connect with our **chakras** one by one.

Root
Place your hands: On your legs.
Envision the color: Red, like hearts.
Ask yourself: "Where do I need more grounding?"
Close your eyes and repeat the phrase in your mind's eye.
Wait for an answer to arrive.
Now, ask yourself: "How can I create this grounding?"

Sacral
Place your hands: On your pelvic area.
Envision the color: Orange, like the fruit.
Ask yourself: "Where do I need more joy?
Close your eyes and repeat the phrase in your mind's eye.
Wait for an answer to arrive.
Now, ask yourself: "How can I create more joy in my life?"

Solar Plexus
Place your hands: On your belly.
Envision the color: Yellow, like a sunrise.
Ask yourself: "Where do I need more courage?
Close your eyes and repeat the phrase in your mind's eye.
Wait for an answer to arrive.
Now, ask yourself: "How can I be more courageous?"

Heart

Place your hands: On your heart.
Envision the color: Green, like a forest
Ask yourself: "Where do I need more love?
Close your eyes and repeat the phrase in your mind's eye.
Wait for an answer to arrive.
Now, ask yourself: "How can I create more love in my life now?"

Throat

Place your hands: On your throat.
Envision the color: Baby blue, like the sky.
Ask yourself: "What words do I need to tell myself now?
Close your eyes and repeat the phrase in your mind's eye.
Wait for an answer to arrive.
Now, ask yourself: "What compliments can I say to myself now?"

Third Eye

Place two fingers: In between your eyebrows.
Envision the color: Dark blue, like the ocean.
Ask yourself: "Where do I need clarity?
Close your eyes and repeat the phrase in your mind's eye.
Wait for an answer to arrive.
Now, ask yourself: "How can I trust my intuition more?"

Crown

Place your hands: On top of your head.
Envision the color: Lavender, like the flower.
Ask yourself: "Where do I need more guidance?
Close your eyes and repeat the phrase in your mind's eye.
Wait for an answer to arrive.
Now, ask yourself: "What do I need guidance with?"

How did the **chakra meditation** feel?

Were you able to **receive answers**?

Chakra Alignment + Affirmations Meditation

This is another lovely **meditation** I created and is a favorite among my students. You will instantly feel the power of the **affirmations being transmitted** into each chakra of your body. To begin, **light a candle**, or *velita*. Put on a meditation song to help you relax and sit in a comfortable spot. Now, let's connect with our **chakras** one by one.

Root Chakra Affirmation
Place your hands: On your legs.
Take a deep breath in and think of: The color red.
Exhale: Slowly.
Repeat this affirmation three times: "I am grounded and safe."
Take: A deep breath in and exhale slowly.
Repeat this affirmation three times: "I trust and know that everything is working out for me."

Sacral Chakra Affirmation
Place your hands: On your pelvis.
Take a deep breath in and think of: The color orange.
Exhale: Slowly.
Repeat this affirmation three times: "I am joy and joy surrounds me."
Take: A deep breath in and exhale slowly.
Repeat this affirmation three times: "I am creative, passionate and I love my life."

Solar Plexus Chakra Affirmation
Place your hands: On your belly.
Take a deep breath in and think of: The color yellow.
Exhale: Slowly.
Repeat this affirmation three times: "I am strong, courageous and powerful."
Take: A deep breath in and exhale slowly.
Repeat this affirmation three times: "I have limitless power in my mind, body and spirit."

Heart Chakra Affirmation
Place your hands: On your heart.
Take a deep breath in and think of: The color green and pink.
Exhale: Slowly.
Repeat this affirmation three times: "I am love and love surrounds me."
Take: A deep breath in and exhale slowly.
Repeat this affirmation three times: "Beautiful love pours through every inch of my being."

Throat Chakra Affirmation
Place your hands: On your throat.
Take a deep breath in think of: The color light blue.
Exhale: Slowly.
Repeat this affirmation three times: "I am a powerful manifestor."
Take: A deep breath in and exhale slowly.
Repeat this affirmation three times: "My gorgeous voice matters in this world."

Third Eye Chakra Affirmation
Place two fingers: On your third eye.
Take a deep breath in and think of: The color dark blue.
Exhale: Slowly.
Repeat this affirmation three times: "I can see my future and it is magnificent."
Take: A deep breath in and exhale slowly.
Repeat this affirmation three times: "I trust my intuition."

Crown Chakra Affirmation
Place your hands: On top of your head.
Take a deep breath in and think of: The color dark purple.
Exhale: Slowly.
Repeat this affirmation three times: "I am divinely guided."
Take: A deep breath in and exhale slowly.
Repeat this affirmation three times: "My angels walk with me."

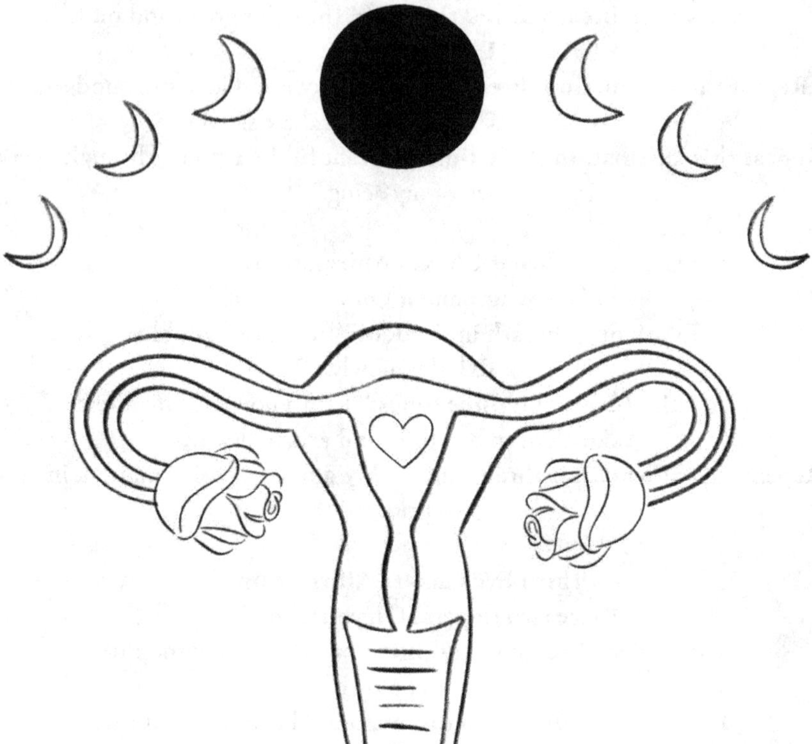

Menstrual Magic

Life Force

"My **menstrual** cycle's blood is **magic**.
It is a life force. I use it to **manifest**."

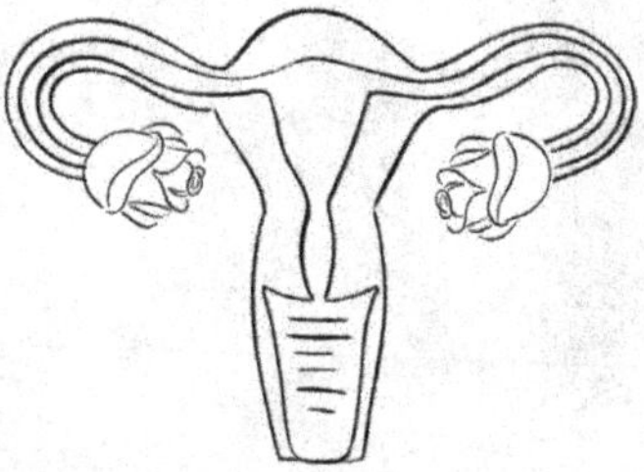

Fuerza Vital

"La sangre de mi ciclo **menstrual** es **mágica**.
Es una fuerza vital. Lo uso para **manifestar.**"

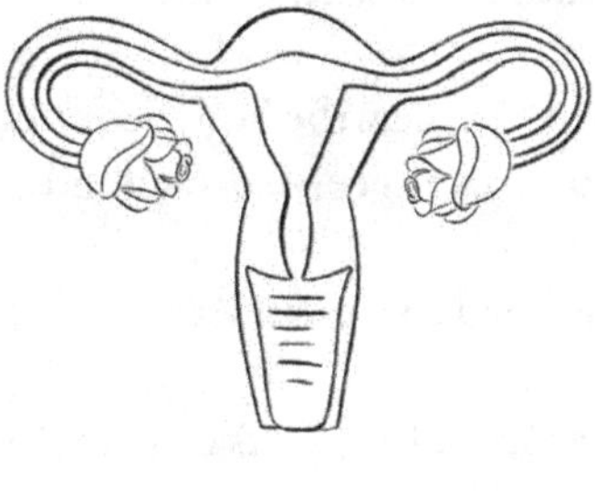

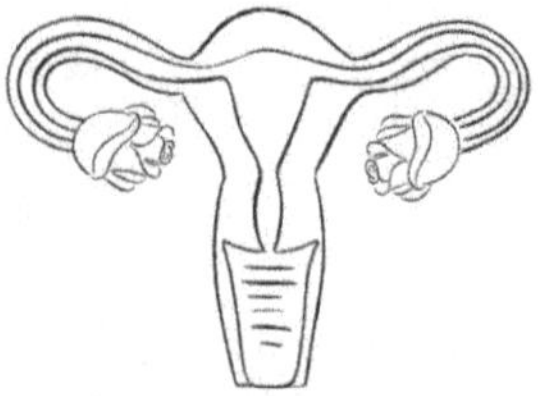

Menstrual Magic: What To Know

Here's what you need to remember:

Your **vagina** is a **portal** that helps to bring life into the world.

Blood is a life force, which can be used to set intentions.
Light a candle, write wishes and add a drop of blood onto the paper.
Fold and then place into a plant and water so it manifests with your energy.

Your period is a time of **release** for the body, mind and spirit.

It is **sacred**.

It is a **highly intuitive** moment.

Think of it as the **death of** old energy and the rebirth of a new you.

During this experience, the body requires extra **rest**
so we can **receive downloads**.

Emotions are amplified so we can see what we need to release.

It is a **potent time for journaling**. Lots of wisdom will come through.

It is beautiful to **embrace** and not force things.

Menstrual Magic: How Your Chakras Become Aligned

Crown Chakra: You're required extra rest and stillness to receive downloads in your dreams and also in a relaxed state.
Menstrual Cycle Detox Symptoms: Headaches, fatigue, vivid dreams.

Third Eye Chakra: Intuition heightens.
Menstrual Cycle Detox Symptoms: Headaches and/or migraines as your intuition is heightening and blockages are being released.

Throat Chakra: Inner communication increases as well as self-awareness.
Menstrual Cycle Detox Symptoms: You are able to hear your inner most thoughts during this time and what no longer serves you. This is an excellent time to journal out those feelings to make sense of this knowledge. Once clarity is established, you can use your throat to communicate to the Universe the abundance and changes you'd like to co-create.

Heart Chakra: Cleanses so all kinds of love can be experienced.
Menstrual Cycle Detox Symptoms: Breast tenderness and swelling. Your self-love is triggered so you can see the degree you love yourself as well as your love for others and your acceptance of it.

Solar Plexus Chakra: Releases limiting beliefs so your limitless power is activated.
Menstrual Cycle Detox Symptoms: Nausea/bloating as any fears and self-doubt are let go and more inner strength and confidence grows.

Sacral Chakra: Power grows as big as the sun, which burns away any opposite energy within.
Menstrual Cycle Detox Symptoms: Cramping happens so that low vibrational energies can exit and joy, passion and creativity can grow.

Root Chakra: The right path becomes clearer and easier to walk through.
Menstrual Cycle Detox Symptoms: Pain in the legs and feet is experienced as trust, grounding and an easier journey opens.

Embrace

"Many of us have been taught our **menstrual cycle** is
unclean and we should dread it versus see the **beauty** in it.
Our menstrual cycle is filled with magic. It is a potent time to **manifest, create and align**. Once you **embrace** this moment, you will feel better and
be able to **harness** this energy and see
how much **power** you have within to
birth creations into your life."

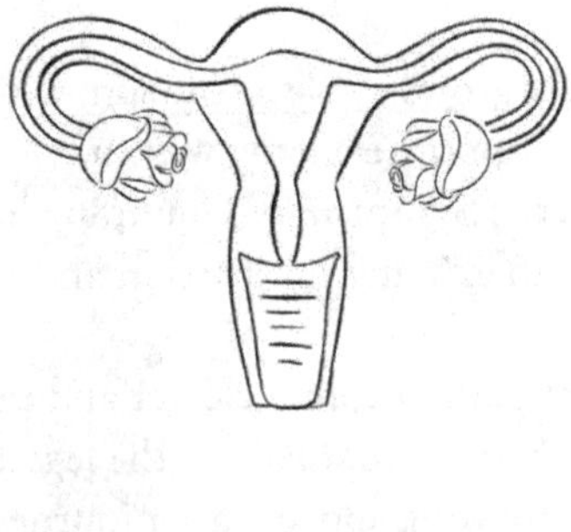

Aceptar

"A muchas de nosotras nos han enseñado que nuestro **ciclo menstrual** es impuro y que debemos temerlo en lugar de ver su **belleza.** Nuestro ciclo menstrual está lleno de magia. Es un momento potente para **manifestar, crear y alinear**. Una vez que **aceptes** este momento, te sentirás mejor y podrás **aprovechar** esta energía y ver cuánto **poder** tienes dentro para hacer nacer **creaciones** en tu vida."

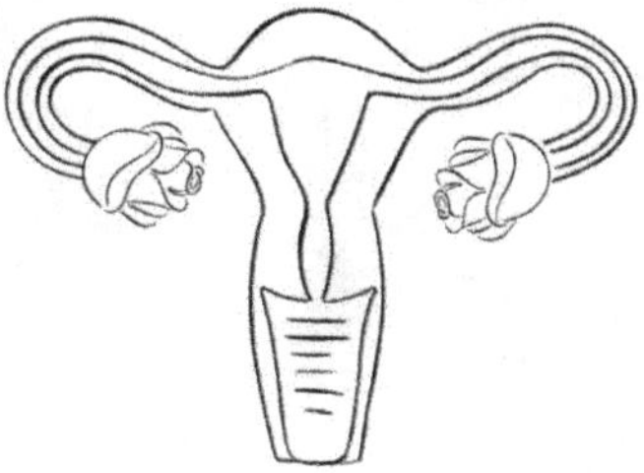

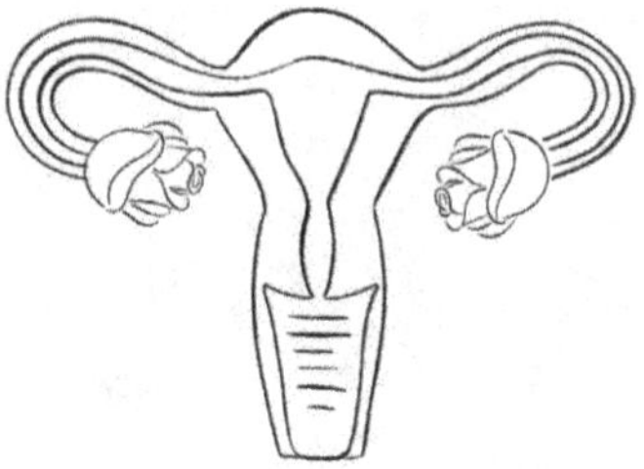

Menopause Magic: What To Know

The Crone is the archetype for **menopause**. This woman has **eternal beauty**. She is wise, powerful and holy. She is one of the **triple goddesses** with the maiden and mother being the other two. Crone stands for **crown chakra**, where **wisdom** lies and the **connection** with the **celestial**. Other terms for this mature goddess that have been misconstrued to keep her from realizing her capabilities is the word "**hag**," which actually means **holy** and comes from the word *hagio*. In the Bible, it means most holy or **saint**. The other is **witch**, which comes from the word **wit** and means **wise**.

Here's what you need to remember:

Menopause is a time of profound **transformation.**

You are able to retain your **wise blood.**

It is time to let go of **attachments.**

A moment to **embrace** one's true essence.

You are moving into another level of **enlightenment** and **self-awareness.**

This is a wonderful time for **renewal.**

Psychic ability **increases.**

You have the ability to **understand life's cycle** better.

Reevaluation of priorities.

The **physical body** experiences many changes.
(**Exercising** will help you create grounding and balance during this rite of passage. Pilates, strength training, yoga and walking are recommended.)

Daily ritual will bring guidance.

Meditation will help you during this beautiful transformation.

Affirmations For Menopause Healing

I am in the midst of a **glorious** transformation.

This is my true **butterfly** era.

I love my **true** essence.

I am a **wise**, wonderful woman.

It is **safe** for me to change.

I **love** this part of my life.

I am **free** of attachments.

My **intuition** is so strong and clear.

I **enjoy** every moment of my life.

To be **alive** is a gift.

This is my moment to **embrace** my true essence.

My body **feels** so healthy.

I am **stronger** than ever.

I am good at **prioritizing** my life.

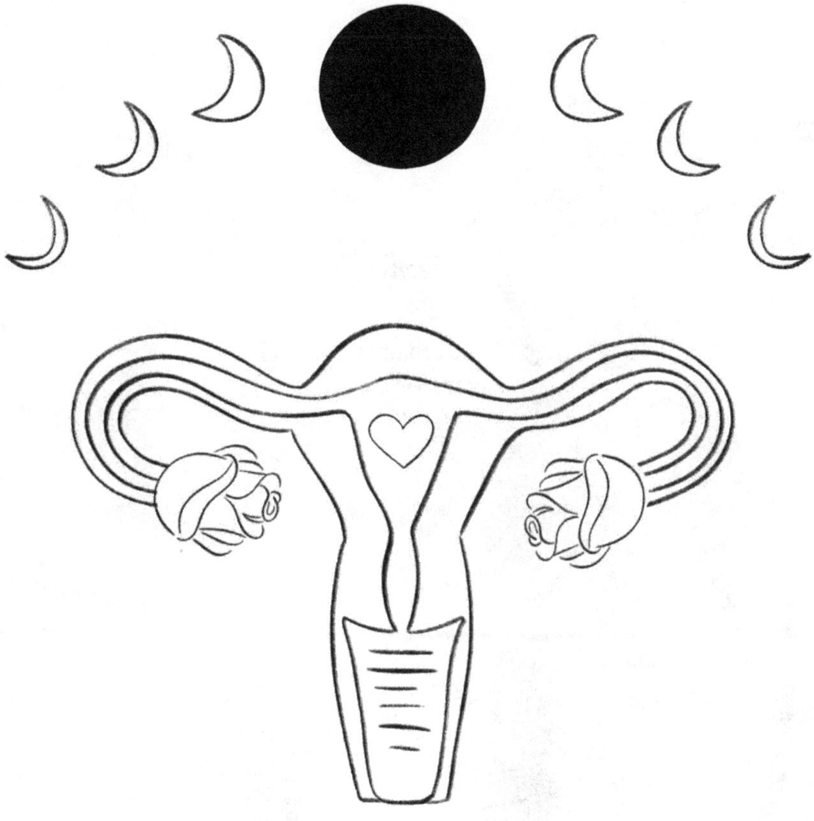

Time

"To **age** is a **gift** many are not given.
Use your **time wisely**."

Tiempo

"**Envejecer** es un **regalo** que muchos no reciben.
Usa tu **tiempo sabiamente.**"

Menopause

"The deepest connection to the **divine feminine** came
when she entered **menopause**, the ultimate definition of a wise woman.
This was not an ending, but a **new beginning** where
her greatest strength and dreams would be witnessed."

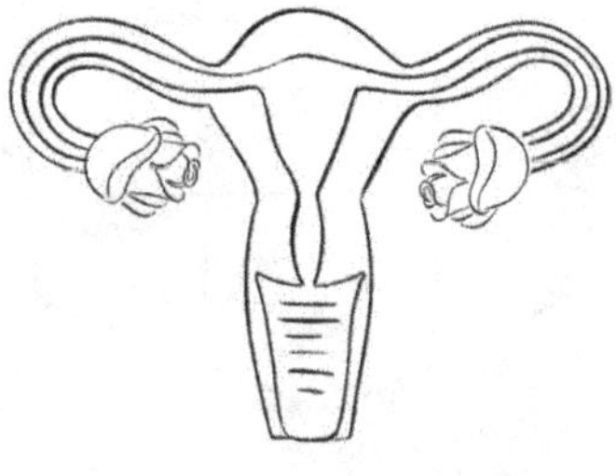

Menopausia

"La conexión más profunda con la **divina femenina** vino cuando entró en la **menopausia**, la definición definitiva de una mujer sabia. Este no fue un final, sino un **nuevo comienzo** donde serían testigos de sus mayores fortalezas y sueños."

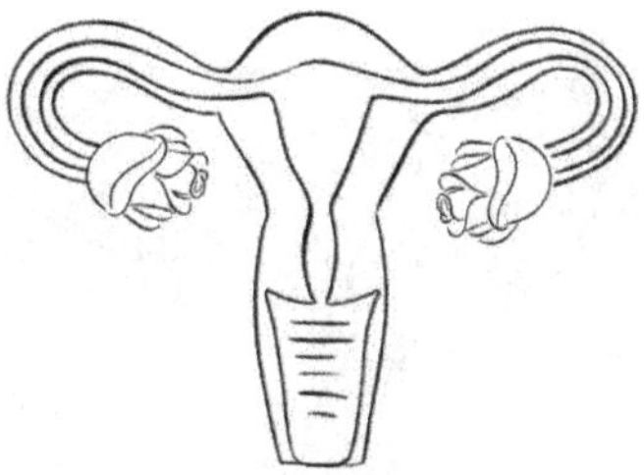

Potent

"In many cultures, entering **menopause** signifies the woman becoming the **most potent** in her magic. She no longer has to shed her **life force** from her **womb** each month but instead can **retain** it. This is **blood filled with wisdom**. This allows her to become her most powerful self. She is now a **medicine woman**, a true healer and guide for other women."

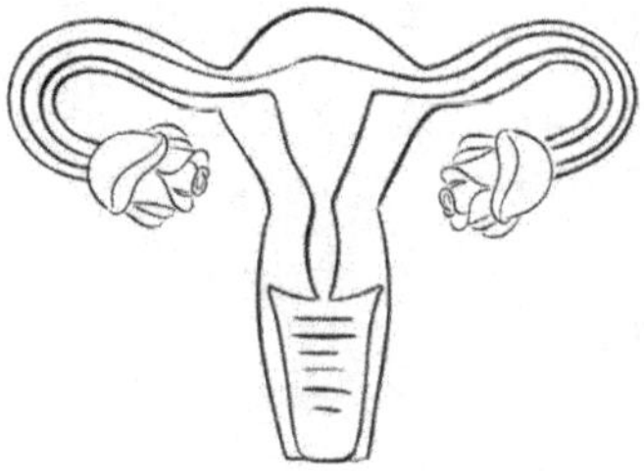

Potente

"En muchas culturas, entrar en la **menopausia** significa que la mujer se convierte en la **más potente** en su magia. Ya no tiene que desprenderse de su **fuerza vital** desde su **útero** cada mes, sino que puede **retenerla.** Esta es **sangre llena de sabiduría.** Esto le permite convertirse más poderosa. Ahora es una **curandera**, una auténtica sanadora y guía para otras mujeres."

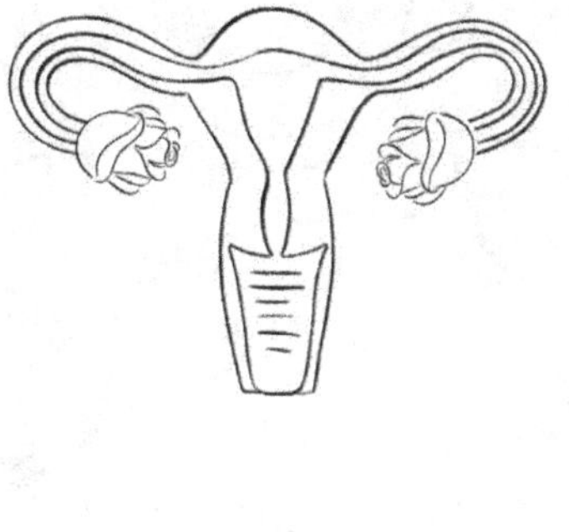

Metamorphosis

I saw the **white strands** growing out of me.
White like **sea foam.**
White like **snow.**
White like a **Magnolia tree.**
I would rise and become a **cloud** one day,
or perhaps a **dove.**

Annie's Favorites:

Plants, Crystals & Recipes

Annie's Favorite House Plants + How to Manifest With Them

Peace Lily
Why: Fosters harmony and balance in your home.
Place: Living room.
Slip a note under: Saying where you'd like harmony and balance.
Check: On the New Moon.

Money Plant
Why: Increases your finances.
Place: Work desk or workplace.
Slip a note under: With a realistic amount of money you'd like now or by the end of year.
Check: On the Full Moon and New Moon.

Lucky Bamboo
Why: Amplifies your good luck.
Place: Work desk or kitchen.
Slip a note under: With one thing you need luck with now. Replace once it has been granted.
Check: On the New Moon.

Snake Plant
Why: Wonderful for protection.
Place: Outside of home as a shield.
Slip a note inside: Thanking your angels for protecting you and your loved ones.
Check: On the Full Moon.

Fiddle Leaf Plant

Why: Brings abundance, fertility and good luck.

Place: By window for sunshine.

Slip a note inside: With intentions you want to birth into the world.

Check: On the New Moon.

Heartleaf Philodendron

Why: Brings love and good health.

Place: In bedroom for healthy love and romance.

Slip a note under: Asking the Universe to bring you what you wish for in love and romance or better than you imagined.

Check: On the Full Moon.

Chinese Evergreen

Why: Doubles your good fortune and prosperity. Also helps to detox your home and bring calm.

Place: In the home, facing southwest.

Slip a note inside: Where you'd like good fortune.

Check: On the New Moon and Full Moon.

Anthurium

Why: Symbolizes love and passion.

Place: Bedroom.

Slip a note inside: Asking the Universe to bring you what you wish for in love or better than you imagined. Make sure you also have your list of attributes you seek in a life partner and a list of attributes you bring to a relationship.

Check: On the New Moon and Full Moon.

Peace Lily

A **Peace Lily** sits by me every morning as I meditate
Its' white petals nudge me to keep **trusting and ground.**
In my work area, the **Money Plant** blooms every
time I believe the Universe is **abundant.**
I place a **Lucky Bamboo** in my bathroom so it
tells me how to stay **attracting** everything I wish for and
the **Heartleaf Philodendron** in my bedroom
reminds me, with its heart-shaped leaves,
to keep my **heart** open to give and receive **love**
unconditionally.
I plant my wishes in them, too. And water my **dreams**
so they **grow** into my life.

Citrine

"My mother gave me a **citrine** ring so
I would never forget I was **born to shine** in this world. "

Citrino

"Mi madre me regaló un anillo de **citrino** para que nunca olvidar que **nací para brillar** en este mundo."

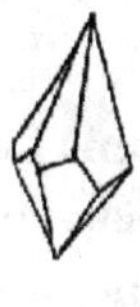

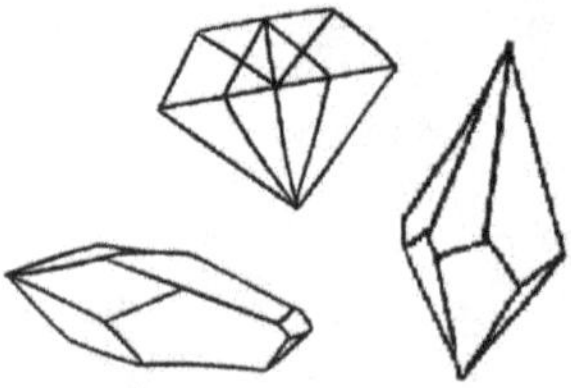

Annie's Favorite Crystals

Amethyst
Why: Brings calming and connection.
Good For: Inner peace and receiving divine messages.

Clear Quartz Crystal
Why: It's the *mamá* of all crystals.
Good For: Detoxing, protection and amplifying your other crystals' powers.

Citrine
Why: Reminds you how limitless and strong you are.
Good For: Powers up your solar plexus and ignites your courage.

Garnet
Why: Makes intentions move faster. Also, brings people back together.
Good For: Connecting with the fire element and tapping into our passion. Brings loved ones back together to meet again. Simply gift to someone before parting.

Lapis Lazuli
Why: Opens your third eye.
Good For: Egyptians once used them as wishing stones. They can be used to heighten your intuition.

Malachite
Why: Makes you prosperous.
Good For: Opening doors to prosperity.

Pink Quartz
Why: Nurtures your self-love.
Good For: Coming back to ourselves and inspiring us to do what makes us feel good.

Onyx
Why: Creates a shield of protection.
Good For: Protecting yourself, loved ones and things of value.

Selenite
Why: Connects you with the moon.
Good For: Moon manifesting, receiving messages from *la luna* and naturally cleanses your other crystals.

Turquoise
Why: Helps you speak your truth and become better at using your voice to manifest.
Good For: The throat chakra.

Tiger's Eye
Why: Used by shamans to travel and creates abundance.
Good For: The root chakra, building a strong foundation and learning to trust your journey.

The Art Of Sacred Geometry

Make a **circle** for endless **abundance**.

Construct a **flower** of life for something to **blossom**.

Use a **hexagon** to hold space for someone or something in **light**.

Draw a **triangle** for celestial communication
so your **angels** can guide you to your future self.

Create a **square** for strength and protection.

Place an intention in a **spiral** for life force and **flow**.

How To Make A Crystal Grid

Crystal grids are a ritual that uses sacred geometry to help you manifest. You set an intention, choose crystals that correlate with that intention and then place them in the form that calls to you. The grid gives extra power to make your intention come to fruition.

Here's a step-by-step guide:

Set your intention for making this grid. It is recommended to write a letter thanking the Universe for giving you this intention or better.

Gather crystals that correlate with your intention.

Choose the sacred geometry form that calls to you. Use your intuition to guide you. Some examples are a **circle** for endless abundance, a **flower of life** for something to blossom, a **hexagon** for holding space, a **triangle** for celestial communication, a **square** for strength and protection and a **spiral** for life force and flow.

Place an **anchor stone** at the center and over your letter. An anchor stone is one that can be larger and represents your intention the most.

Next, **start placing the crystals** in the shape you choose.

For **extra energy**, you can place other lovely objects like a photo, flowers, leaves or even candles around to bring more beautiful energy to your intention.

Lastly, it is time to **activate your crystal grid**. You can do this by lighting a candle and praying, or you can sit next to it and meditate to see if you receive messages. Another lovely way is to play sound bowls for it.

Revisit your grid every Full Moon by burning sage to release any blockages that might surround your intention.

Circle Grid

Why: To make an intention come in full circle.
How: Place crystals around a circle. Then, inside, place the intention you'd like to activate here.
Revisit: Full and New Moons to see how it is progressing.
Reflect: Write in your journal how it is materializing and what other actions you can do to make it come into fruition.

Flower Grid

Why: To make an intention blossom.
How: Place crystals over flower shape. Then, inside, place the intention you'd like to activate here.
Revisit: Full and New Moons to see how it is progressing.
Reflect: Write in your journal how it is materializing and what other actions you can do to make it come into fruition.

Hexagon Grid

Why: To hold space for an intention.
How: Place crystals over hexagon shape. Then, inside, place the intention you'd like to activate here.
Revisit: Full and New Moons to see how it is progressing.
Reflect: Write in your journal how it is materializing and what other actions you can do to make it come into fruition.

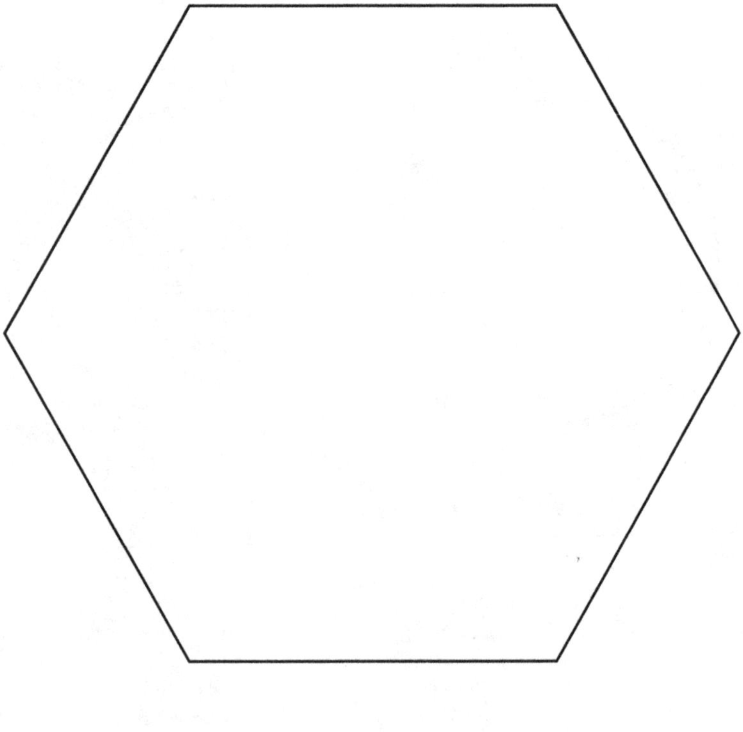

Triangle Grid

Why: To receive guidance on an intention.
How: Place crystals in a triangle shape. Then, inside, place the intention you'd like to activate here.
Revisit: Full and New Moons to see how it is progressing.
Reflect: Write in your journal how it is materializing and what other actions you can do to make it come into fruition.

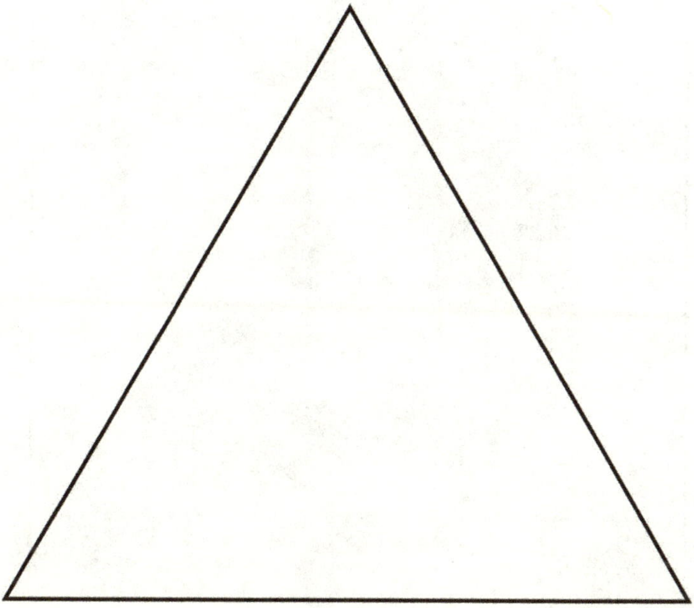

Square Grid

Why: To protect and strengthen an intention.
How: Place crystals in a square shape. Then, inside, place the intention you'd like to activate here.
Revisit: Full and New Moons to see how it is progressing.
Reflect: Write in your journal how it is materializing and what other actions you can do to make it come into fruition.

Spiral Grid

Why: To create flow for an intention.
How: Place crystals in a spiral shape. Then, inside, place the intention in the center of the spiral to activate it.
Revisit: Full and New Moons to see how it is progressing.
Reflect: Write in your journal how it is materializing and what other actions you can do to make it come into fruition.

Annie's Kitchen Magic: Recipes And More

These are some beloved recipes I've learned from
wise women along the way.

The Kitchen Magic: Apple
Do: Place a coin on top or next to the apple.
Why: Brings you money and helps you save.

The Kitchen Magic: Apple pie
Do: Place a fresh apple pie by a window.
Why: It calls in love.

The Kitchen Magic: Bowl of oranges
Do: Make a bowl of lovely oranges in your kitchen.
Why: It calls in abundance and joy.

The Kitchen Magic: Cinnamon
Do: Boil some cinnamon.
Stand in front of it and say where you'd like some abundance.
Why: Calls in abundance.

The Kitchen Magic: Eggs
Do: Place 2 eggs (uncooked) under your bed to remove bad energy in romance, sleeping and health. Leave for 7 days and then toss out.
Why: Restores the peace.

The Kitchen Magic: Lemon and salt
Do: Put half a lemon slice in a bowl of water and a dash of salt to remove negative energy in your space. Place anywhere it feels heavy.
Leave for 3 days and toss out. Repeat if necessary.
Why: Cleanses the energy in your space.

The Kitchen Magic: Sage your kitchen with the windows open.
Do: Open the windows when you sage to clear out the energy from your space.
Say, "*I release blocks and replace them with blessings.*"
Why: Kitchens symbolize health, abundance and wealth in Feng shui. It is where we gather for nourishment.

The Kitchen Magic: Salt
Do: Take salt into the shower and scrub yourself.
Why: It helps to release stress and cleanses your aura.
Repeat this affirmation as you do it:
"*I release what doesn't serve me.*"

The Kitchen Magic: Stove
Do: Turn on all 4 burners for 1 minute.
Why: It shifts the energy and brings good news and money.

The Kitchen Magic: Tea
Do: Drink it while reading intentions.
Why: Helps you receive visions and information on how to co-create it.

The Kitchen Magic: Bay leaves
Do: Toss them in food or burn them alone.
Why: Ancient Greeks used it because they saw the magic in it.
Bay leaves in food helps your health, strength and ignites passion.
Burning one helps cleanse spaces and release inflammation.

The Kitchen Magic: Stand before any fruit, vegetable or legumes boiling in water.
Do: This exercise opens your third eye as water is connected to your psychic flow and seeing hidden truths.
Why: Delivers messages to you and increases your intuition.

Divination

"I grew up watching the women in my family toss **bay leaves** into food as they cooked. Later, in my life I would learn to use these very leaves to write my **wishes** on because they made them **manifest**. Centuries before we even existed, Greek women, mostly the **oracles**, would **eat** and **burn** them inhaling in their smoke to open the doors to **prophecy** and **divination**. Delphi, was one of the most famous sites where kings, philosophers and pilgrims came to hear from these **wise women**."

Adivinación

"Crecí viendo a la mujeres de mi familia tirar **hojas de laurel** a las comidas mientras cocinaban. Más adelante, en mi vida aprendería a utilizar estas mismas hojas para escribir mis **deseos** porque los hacían **manifiestar**. Siglos antes de que existiéramos, las mujeres griegas, en su mayoría **oráculos**, los **comían** y **quemaban** inhalando su humo para abrir las puertas a la **profecía** y la **adivinación**. Delfos, fue uno de los sitios más famosos donde reyes, filósofos y peregrinos acudían para escuchar a estas **sabias mujeres.**"

Meditative

"**Cooking** can be a **meditative** practice and,
when done with boiling water,
it can **open** up your third eye to bring you **messages**."

Meditativa

"**Cocinar** puede ser una práctica **meditativa** y,
cuando se hace con agua hirviendo,
puede **abrir** tu tercer ojo para enviarte **mensajes.**"

Black Bean Magic

The day I found out
I would be **married**,
we sat **separating**
an entire **bag**
of **black beans** together.

My 10-year-old **hands**
molded little **mountains** with them.
The good beans **rising** high
like **Mt. Everest.**

The "**uncookable**" ones,
according to my **great aunt**,
tossed into a lower elevation
"no name" **heap.**

My future **love life**
would resemble these two **piles.**

And on occasion,
I'd give a **bad bean**
a chance, and just as she had **warned**,
would leave a **bad taste** in my mouth.

That day, she told me my **future.**
We lined the **perfect beans**
before a **pot of water**,
and with one **gentle** hand swipe,
they **dove** in, making tiny splashes.

That's when she reached for
a giant wooden **spatula** and
began stirring and **speaking**.

"You know, there's a **book** about
your entire **life** and the man
you're going to **marry**," she said.
"His **name** is in there."

"That's how your mom and dad **met**.
That's how I met my **husband**.
It's in the **book**.
God has the book."

25 years later, this **book** would find
its way back into my **life**, but this time,
not from my great **aunt** a devoted Catholic who prays
the rosary, has a painting of Jesus at **The Last Supper**,
a few small statues of saints like **St. Martin**,
St. Lazarus and a bottle of holy water
at her dresser.

This book, a **psychic** would mention to me,
had the name of my **future** husband in it.
Only now there would be no **black beans**,
just a bowl of **water** in front of us.
She swirled back and forth just like my great
aunt had done,
handing me his **initial**
from a book called the **Akashic records**.
I would **tell** you more,
but I won't **spill the beans**.

Perfect Blend

"I am the ***sazón completa***
and I am the perfect blend of love, light and stars."

Mezcla Perfecta

"Soy la ***sazón completa***
y soy la mezcla perfecta de amor, luz y estrellas."

What Is Sazón Completa?

Sazón Completa is a go-to seasoning blend, commonly used in Cuban and Caribbean cooking.

The Sazón Completa

I paint my nails red hot
like ***chile* peppers**,
lick my lashes with a coat of mascara
extra black the color of ***frijoles negros***,
tint my lips the hue of **sweet *mamey***.

Estoy sola pero no mal acompañada.
I beautify myself for myself
because I am una ***belleza*** and
so are you, ***mujer***.

I **salsa dance** my hips into
a white eyelet dress,
slip on **cognac**-toned cowboy boots,
the ones I imagine my family wearing
in Pinar del Rio, **Cuba**.

Estoy sola pero no mal acompañada.
I take myself for a sunset **summer**
stroll through a hot humid **Central Park**
because I am the occasion to go out and
so are you, *mujer*.

I buy myself a glass of **Rosé** and
sip in **celebration** that I am here.
I am the **love** I seek.
I am the **freedom** my ancestors fought for.
I am the **peace** and **good health** I learned
no one could give me but me.
Estoy sola pero no mal acompañada.
You see, I am the ***sazón completa*** and
so are you, ***mujer***.

3 Recipes To Make Life *Dulce* By The Day

1| *Primero*
Go to a Cuban restaurant.
Order from their window or *ventanita*
a *pastelito de* **guava** and a ***cafe*** *con leche.*
Submerge part of the **dessert** in the caffeine concoction
Then, slowly pull it up to **taste** and feel
the **tropical deliciousness** on your tongue.
Let it linger for a moment like a bee on a flower
so the guava opens you to **love, prosperity and good luck.**

2 | *Segundo*
For protection, cleansing and blessings,
I grant you my grandmother **Yuya's recipe**:
1 large *lata* or can of Ancel's ***dulce coco.***
It can only be Ancel, according to my abuela.
2 cans of ***leche evaporada*** or evaporated milk.
2 *ramos de* ***canela*** or 2 cinnamon sticks.
½ *taza de* ***azucar*** or cup of sugar.
Fuego lento or cook it slowly all together
por tres horas (for 3 hours.)
Keep stirring.
Now in this mixing, **meditate.**
In between, **write out intentions**, read them out loud
and **take *cucharadas*, or spoonfuls, of the sweetness.**

3 | *Tercero*
Lastly, book a ticket to **Spain**
for the best ***Arroz Con Leche.***
This ***dulce*** brings you
abundance and **fertility** to birth whatever is in your heart
With every mouthful, you will manifest your dreams.
Simply envision your best future self in every bite.

Annie's Wise Women Home Magic

These are some lovely Feng shui tips
I've learned from wise women along the way.

The Home Magic: Broom
Do: Broom your space for quick energy cleanse.
Why: Increases your joy, releases anxiety and helps abundance arrive.

The Home Magic: Donation box
Do: Place unused items in this box.
Why: Removes stagnant energy and helps you receive the abundance you wish for and more.

The Home Magic: Feng shui bells
Do: Hang on front door to clean energy as you and your guests go in and out.
Why: Increases creativity and flow of money.

The Home Magic: Fountain
Do: Place a fountain at the entrance of your home or near it.
Why: Cleanses the energy in your space and brings wealth.

The Home Magic: Ganesha
Do: Place a Ganesha photo or figurine in your space.
Why: Helps to remove obstacles.

The Home Magic: Happy Buddha
Do: Place a Happy Buddha in your space.
Why: Increases joy and happiness.

The Home Magic: Jasmine incense
Do: Burn it.
Why: Helps attract love and romance.

The Home Magic: Lavender oil
Do: Sprinkle on bedsheets and pillows.
Why: Helps you get a good night's rest.

The Home Magic: Mirror
Do: Place a mirror at your work desk.
Why: Increases creativity and flow of money.

Food Is Medicine

We know **food** has the power to **heal** us in many ways.
Certain foods can also benefit your **chakras** and help you feel your best.
I compiled a **list of foods** and how they can help **power up** certain **chakras.** Take a look.

Root Chakra
Eat: Red fruits and veggies.
Grocery List: Beetroot, strawberries, radishes and tomatoes.
Root foods can help you feel grounded.
Some examples are carrots, malanga, potatoes and parsnips.
Purpose: Sparks grounding, reminds you that you are safe, secure and your basic needs are being met.

Sacral Chakra
Eat: Orange fruits and veggies.
Grocery List: Carrots, mangoes, oranges, papaya, passion fruit, squash and sweet potatoes.
Purpose: Invigorates your joy, creativity and pleasure.

Solar Plexus Chakra
Eat: Yellow fruits, spices and veggies.
Grocery List: Bananas, corn, ginger, lemons, mangoes, pineapple, turmeric, pepper and squash.
Purpose: Powers up your strength, inner confidence and reminds you of your limitless abilities to achieve.

Heart Chakra
Eat: Green fruits, veggies and herbs.
Grocery List: Apples, avocado, broccoli, celery, cucumber, kale, lettuce, limes, peppers and spinach.
Purpose: Opens your heart to give and receive love freely without expectations.

Throat Chakra
Eat: Blue fruits, veggies and teas.
Grocery List: Blueberries, lots of tea and water.
Purpose: Aligns your inner and outer voice so that you can manifest. Remember that both need to be aligned in order to reel in your intentions.

Third Eye Chakra
Eat: Indigo fruits and veggies.
Grocery List: Blackberries, blue potato, black currants, elderberries and figs.
Purpose: Opens your all knowing eye and psychic antenna to bring you clarity and the ability to see hidden truths.

Crown Chakra
Eat: Purple foods.
Grocery List: Cabbage, eggplant grapes, fig, plums, purple carrots and purple potatoes.
Purpose: Connects with you the Universe to bring guidance, celestial wisdom and direction.

Closing Wisdom

"A birthmark in Spanish is called ***lunar***,
which means connected to the moon. If you look close enough,
you'll see a piece of the **solar system** on your skin.
Here, you will find all the **wise women** you once were and still are."

"Una marca de nacimiento en español se llama **lunar,**
que significa conectada a la luna. Si miras más cerca,
verás una parte del **sistema solar** en tu piel. Aquí encontrarás
todas las **mujeres sabias** que alguna vez fuiste y aún eres."

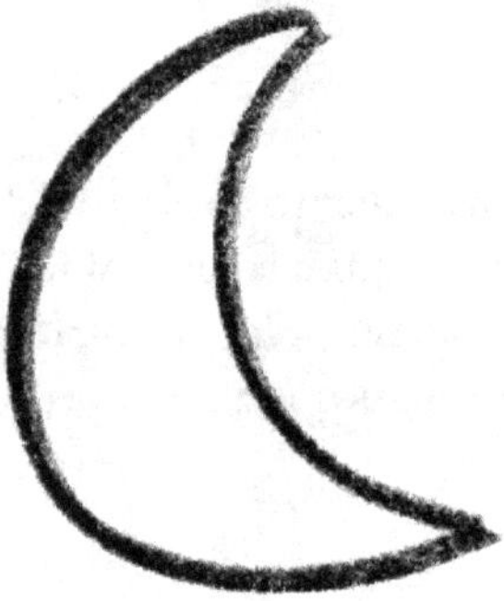

Birthmark, *Lunar*

A birthmark in Spanish is called ***lunar***, which means connected to the moon. If you look close enough, you'll see a piece of the **solar system** on your skin. Here you will find all the **wise women** you once were and still are. Some birthmarks show you a **map** of the planets, moons and stars orbiting around you. Other *lunares* are **tiny chapters** from your other lives. Some pinpoint the exact area in your **physical body** from another life where you received an injury or a trauma you died from. There are stories of people recognizing the **reincarnated** after seeing their *lunar*. If two people have matching *lunares*, it means they most likely traveled together at one point. If you are ready, press on your birthmark and ask it a question. It will tell you about a former life or why you have this beautiful little **kiss of a constellation** on you.

Timeline

"My **future** is a beautiful **story** I get to **write**."

Línea De Tiempo

"Mi **futuro** es una hermosa **historia** que puedo **escribir**."

Stars

Within your walls,
you carry **extraordinary wisdom.**
You are a **wise woman**, or *mujer sabia.*
And when things are unclear or life feels heavy,
step outside and **look up** at all the wise women above you shining as **stars.**
Then, ask them what to do.
They will answer you.
They always do.

Leave A Review:

I would love to know your thoughts on how
My Little Spiritual Book: Rituals, Poems & Practices for Enlightenment
helped you or someone you care about. Leave me a review
wherever you purchased this book so we can
further connect and continue to inspire
others to believe in their magic.

Acknowledgments

I would love to thank my parents, **George** and **Carmen.** Thanks for catching my falls, lifting me back up and guiding my eyes back to look up at the sun. I love you both infinitely.

My wombmates: **George**, **Arthur** and **Melissa** for existing and believing in me as a writer.

Elmo for sending me signs and messages from Heaven. Since you've been gone, I understand what stars are now.

Petunia for your little soulful spirit, magic fairy dust and helping me write Book 2.

Annie the Alchemist followers for your hearts of gold and unwavering support.

My beloved dear *amigas* for being second sisters to me and continuously getting me back on the path when I veered off.

My beautiful advanced readers. Thank you for taking time to read and give me your feedback. I am beyond grateful to each of you and for your support. I reached out to you because you are an inspiration to me: **Ana Flores, Alejandra Ramos, Aurora Dominguez, Alex Segura, Cata Balzano, Jo' Martinez, Lucy Lopez, Rebecca Arroyo, Shirley Velasquez, Taimara Dietsch, Tiffany Arocha, Zayda Rivera.**

Indie Earth Publishing for helping me put my second book out into the world.

All the readers that find their inner wise women through this book.

Annie Vazquez has also written and been featured in:

My Little Prayer Book:
75 Prayers, Poems & Mantras for Illumination (2023)

The Abundance Journal (2024)

The Spell Jar: Poetry for the Modern Witch (2022)

Love Letters To The 305 (2023)

Glow: Self-Care Poetry for the Soul (2023)

The Spell Jar: Book of Shadows (2023)

A Winter's Warmth: Short Stories To Keep Out The Cold (2023)

The Spell Jar: Piercing the Veil (2024)

About the Author

Annie Vazquez is the author of *My Little Prayer Book: 75 Prayers, Poems and Mantras for Illumination*. She is poet, writer and former journalist, featured in the Miami Herald, Refinery29, NBC6 and Good Morning America. Annie is known for pioneering Miami fashion blogging through her award-winning blog The Fashion Poet, which has been seen in countless glossies, like Vogue Brasil. Brands like Mercedes Benz, American Express, Coach, H&M, Veuve Cliquot and several tourism boards are just a few that have hired her. Her other brainchild, Annie the Alchemist, is an online wellness shop that offers tools and meditations, reiki and sound bowl healing. Annie is certified by Deepak Chopra's Chopra Meditation School, and her shop has been featured on People Español, Elite Daily, Latin Biz, Parents and Time Out Magazine. Annie has published a variety of ebooks on self-love and wellness and has created a bestselling affirmation deck titled *Affirmations for Abundance.* Her poetry has been featured in a variety of anthologies and publications, including *The Spell Jar* Poetry Series and *Glow: Self-Care Poetry for the Soul,* among others. When Annie is not writing, she is hanging out with her BFFs, Elmo and Petunia, and traveling the world.

Connect with Annie on Instagram:
@anniewriteswords / @thefashionpoet / @anniethealchemist

www.annievazquez.com

About Indie Earth Publishing

Indie Earth Publishing is an author-first, independent co-publishing company based in Miami, FL. A publisher for writers founded by a writer, Indie Earth offers the support and technical assistance of traditional publishing to writers without asking them to compromise their creative freedom. Each Indie Earth Author is a part of an inspired and creative community that only keeps growing. For more titles from Indie Earth, or to inquire about publication, visit:

indieearthbooks.com

Instagram: @indieearthbooks

For inquiries, please email:
indieearthpublishinghouse@gmail.com

Printed in the USA
CPSIA information can be obtained
at www.ICGtesting.com
CBHW030334091124
17085CB00004B/6

9 798991 216456